SOCRATIC SEMINARS AND LITERATURE CIRCLES FOR MIDDLE AND HIGH SCHOOL ENGLISH

Victor J. Moeller

Marc V. Moeller

EYE ON EDUCATION
6 DEPOT WAY WEST, SUITE 106
LARCHMONT, NY 10538
(914) 833–0551
(914) 833–0761 fax
www.eyeoneducation.com

Library of Congress Cataloging-in-Publication Data

Moeller, Marc V., 1970–
    Socratic seminars and literature circles for middle and high school English / by Marc V. Moeller and Victor J. Moeller.
        p.   cm.
    Includes bibliographical references.
    ISBN 1-930556-22-5
    1. English language—Study and teaching (Middle school)—United States. 2. English language—Study and teaching (Secondary school)—United States. 3. Questioning. 4. Group reading—United States. I. Moeller, Victor J., 1937– II. Title.

    LB1631.M515 2002
    428′.007′273—dc21

                                                                                    2001040351

10 9 8 7 6 5 4 3 2 1

Editorial and production services provided by
Richard H. Adin Freelance Editorial Services
52 Oakwood Blvd., Poughkeepsie, NY 12603-4112
(845-471-3566)

Also Available from EYE ON EDUCATION

High School English Teacher's Guide to Active Learning
by Victor J. Moeller and Marc V. Moeller

Middle School English Teacher's Guide to Active Learning
by Marc V. Moeller and Victor J. Moeller

**An English Teacher's Guide to Performance
Tasks and Rubrics: High School**
by Amy Benjamin

**An English Teacher's Guide to Performance
Tasks and Rubrics: Middle School**
by Amy Benjamin

**Standards-Based Activities with Scoring Rubrics:
Middle and High School English
Vol. 1: Performance-Based Portfolios
Vol. 2: Performance-Based Projects**
by Jackie Glasgow, Editor

Writing in the Content Areas
by Amy Benjamin

The Paideia Classroom
by Terry Roberts with Laura Billings

Collaborative Learning in Middle and Secondary Schools
by Dawn M. Snodgrass and Mary M. Bevevino

Teaching English in the Block
by Joseph Stzepek, Jeffry Newton, and Dan Walker, Jr.

Socratic Seminars in the Block
by Wanda H. Ball and Pam Brewer

Teacher Leader
by Thomas Poetter and Bernard Badiali

Personalized Instruction
by James W. Keefe and John M. Jenkins

Coaching and Mentoring First Year and Student Teachers
by India J. Podsen, and Vicki M. Denmark

Performance Standards and Authentic Learning
by Allan A. Glatthorn

ACKNOWLEDGMENTS

"We are as pygmies standing on the shoulders of giants."

Saint Bernard of Clairveaux

I must give credit where it is due. Much of what I know about the Socratic method of teaching, I learned during my 14 years as an in-service instructor (1967–81) and Area Director for the Great Books Foundation and from my mentor Mortimer Adler. While most of the ideas that I present here are my own in that I have developed and refined them over the last 35 years in the classroom, the seminal ideas are found in Adler's writings and the training manuals of the Great Books Foundation. As I mention in the Preface, no book by itself can make one a Socratic teacher. Only a good training course makes that difference. I recommend two:

- The Basic Leader Training Course of the Great Books Foundation, Chicago. For the national schedule of training dates and sites near you check www.greatbooks.org.

- The program of the National Council for Excellence in Critical Thinking www.criticalthinking.org/ncect.nci.

MEET THE AUTHORS

Victor J. Moeller has taught rhetoric, American English and world literature, journalism, creative writing and other courses at several high schools. He was an in-service field instructor and Area Director for the Great Books Foundation for 14 years. During that time he conducted the Great Books Foundation (Chicago) Basic and Advanced Leader Training course in 36 states. He has masters degrees in English and education. With his son Marc, he is the coauthor of *High School English Teacher's Guide to Active Learning* and *Middle School English Teacher's Guide to Active Learning.* Victor Moeller currently teaches at Jacobs High School in Algonquin, Illinois, and may be reached by e-mail at moeller@mc.net or at http://user.mc.net/~moeller/.

Marc V. Moeller has taught courses at high schools and middle schools ranging from AP English (rhetoric and English literature) to English as a second language. He has a master's degree in education from National Louis University of Chicago. He states that the greatest influence on his teaching career has been Victor Moeller, his father and mentor. Marc Moeller currently teaches English at Barrington Middle School in Illinois, and may be reached by e-mail at marcanna@chicago.avenew.com.

TABLE OF CONTENTS

PREFACE

"Learning is not a spectator sport."

- Teachers talk too much.

- Telling a student to think is like telling a pig to fly.

- There can be no learning without discipline.

- The school that fails to teach thinking, fails in everything.

- The student, not the teacher, is the primary agent of learning.

- Nothing is more daunting for a teacher than to get a student to think.

- Teaching is not chiefly about passing out information.

- The best kind of discipline is to engage students in engrossing activities.

- If thinking was easy, there would be more of it.

- The role of the teacher is to uncover the question that the answer hides.

- Thoughtful teachers create thoughtful students.

- Thinking is a skill that has to be practiced daily like playing a piano.

- Authentic learning begins when teachers confront students with problems about meaning—real questions—that demand solutions.

Dear Colleague,

If you agree with most, or at least some, of the above statements, you have found a kindred spirit. As I shake your hand and get a chair for you, let me explain briefly how this book will help you become a better teacher. Everything in this text is based on the assumption that students, not teachers, are the primary agents in learning. The corollary is that authentic learning is active learning. The consequence is that students become responsible for their own learning.

I have been writing this book in my imagination for the last 30 years. It describes, illustrates, and explains how to engage your students in a variety of active learning activities. However, just as no book on tennis, for example, can make you a good tennis player, neither can a book on active learning, by itself, make you a proficient teacher. Nevertheless, with sustained effort, practice, experimentation, guidance, and willingness to learn from your mistakes, you can learn how to become an active learner along with your students.

To get a better idea of what I do with my students, check out my English Student HomePage (http://user.mc.net/~moeller/). If you have questions, comments, or suggestions, I would love to hear from you since it is, after all, for teachers like you that this book has been assembled (moeller@mc.net).

Finally, while I teach high school students, my son Marc, teaches in middle school. For half of these active learning strategies, he has provided corresponding, classroom-tested, and refined materials for grades six through eight.

1

Two Models of Teaching and Overview

If Good Teaching Is a Dialogue, Why Does the Little-Red-School-House Method Continue to Dominate?

Robert Benchley once remarked that "There are two kinds of people, those who classify things and those who don't." Since I belong to the first group, I tend to classify teachers according to those who still employ the little-red-school-house model of learning by lecturing and those who daily engage their students in active learning. I do so not only because most of my former teachers assumed that they were the most important part of the learning process but also because the lecture method dominates among too many teachers even today. In contrast, the so-called Socratic teacher knows that the student is the most important part of the learning process.

Take my high school American literature teacher, Mr. Prosser. He began most lessons by stating the objective—"By the end of this class you will be able to identify the characteristics of the *code hero* in Hemingway"—and then, anticipating the so-what-looks on our faces, explained the relevance or importance of this knowledge: "Hemingway's concept of the *code hero* will give you standards by which to judge your own ideas of heroism." The class proceeded as a lecture. Mr. Prosser knew what a code hero was and he was going to tell us, tell us that he told us, and then ask us to tell him what he had told us. Our job as students was to *pay attention*, that is, to be receptive and passive and to take careful, detailed notes. We were not to interrupt his lecture with comments. We were allowed to ask questions for elementary clarification, for example, "What do you mean by pragmatic?" or "Who is James L. Roberts?" or "Why do you call this stuff 'literary criticism'?" His authority was supreme, his answers all we needed to know on those subjects. After all, he had a master's degree.

1

His lessons concluded with an objective test. "I am the tester, and you are the testees," he would say, and never would we break from those roles. However, "to be fair"—another of his pet phrases—he "entertained" questions before the test. If we had none, Mr. Prosser judged his lesson a success. In the end, we were to trust that Mr. Prosser knew best even when we did not know what he was talking about. "Someday you will understand, and all will be clear," he would reassure us.

What I eventually came to understand, thanks to my college contemporary literature professor, Kenelm Basil, was that there was a better way to teach. Mr. Basil was a Socratic teacher if ever there was one. He began each lesson not by telling us what we were going to learn (he was not certain that we would learn anything although that was, of course, his fondest hope) but by posing a major problem about the meaning the day's assigned reading. He began always with a basic question of interpretation, wrote it on the board, and then asked each of us to write down our own initial answers on scrap paper. For example, "According to Vonnegut's story, *Harrison Bergeron*, is the desire to excel as strong as the tendency to be mediocre?" Because he kept his opinions to himself—he was not a participant but a leader—and asked only follow-up questions on our comments, Mr. Basil convinced us over time that he really did not have a single correct answer in mind. Indeed, the class soon realized that more than one correct answer was possible because evidence from the story supported both sides of the issue. In short, our teacher began the discussion with a real question, the answer to which he himself was uncertain.

As students, we had to be active: clarify our answers, test others' answers for supporting evidence, resolve conflicting answers with evidence, and listen for more opinions. Learning in Mr. Basil's classroom was not about receiving ideas but about wrestling with them. The test of truth was reason and evidence, not teacher authority. The lesson concluded with a resolution activity since, after all, questions are quests for answers. We were asked to review our original responses and then to write a one-page essay stating our comprehensive answer to the basic question. Mr. Basil strove not for group consensus or truth by vote, but for individual understandings: "Given the answers that you have just heard in discussion, what now is your solution?"

Liberation at last! I no longer had to sit dutifully silent while someone told me what I could just as easily have read for myself, found in a library, or researched on the Internet. I no longer had to parrot the teacher's interpretations. More important, Mr. Basil challenged me to think independently and to become responsible for my ideas. The responsibility for learning had been placed in my hands and along with it, the joy and personal satisfaction of arriving at my own insights. I had learned to live with doubt and to uncover questions that answers hide. In short, I learned how to learn.

Do not misunderstand. Most so-called Socratic teachers do not conduct discussions the way Mr. Basil did. Many have not mastered the art of fostering reflective, independent thinking. Such teachers confuse the right to express an opinion with the notion that any opinion can be right. Toleration of any and all ideas becomes the goal, and brainstorming—that pathetic analogy—gets enthroned as the method. As one mindless person put it, "Don't we all know that everything is relative and that there are no absolutes?" Except, of course, his opinion.

Others, the pseudo-Socratic teachers, offer little more than a disguised lecture. These teachers pretend to conduct open discussions but have specific answers in mind. They tip their hands in several ways: by asking leading questions—"How can you honestly think Vonnegut would agree with you?" by allowing opinions that they agree with to go unchallenged or unsubstantiated; by developing a single line of argument or a single side of an issue; by injecting their opinions into the discussion—"I believe that you have all overlooked important information on page six;" by commenting on student answers—"That's very good, James. I'm so proud of you" or, "Maria, I think you had better reconsider your answer. You are missing something;" and finally, by attempting to arrive at group consensus—"I would like to see a show of hands. How many think the desire to excel is as strong as the tendency to be mediocre."

If what I have said about these would-be Socratic teachers is not true, how else are we to explain these examples of common student and teacher behaviors?

Teacher: "Whenever I try to have discussion, my students clam up. Only one or two contribute. They just don't get the point. I *have* to tell them."

Student: "My answer is correct, isn't it Mrs. Jones?"

Teacher: "Discussion is a waste of time. I have to cover the curriculum."

Student: "But Mrs. Jones, what *is* the right answer?"

Teacher: "My students' test scores have to improve. I don't have time for the luxury of endless discussions. I have 130 students. Get real."

Student: "Why do you keep asking questions when you know the answers?"

Teacher: "Students don't know how to ask good questions and anyway, discussions are just too messy."

Student: "Just let me alone and give me my C. I don't mess up your class."

Teacher: "My students cannot be trusted to think for themselves.
They keep coming up with silly answers."

But isn't that just the point? The lecturing teacher fails to understand that wrong answers are a necessary part of the learning process when real thinking takes place. In contrast, the authentic Socratic teacher recognizes and accepts false turns and "silly" answers as inevitable when students have the freedom to be wrong—*and* right. After all, thinking IS difficult and students resist it like a plague. Any teacher will recognize immediately the common cop-outs: "I don't know" or "Why did you call on me?" or "I wasn't doing anything" or "Who cares?" or "What difference does it make?" and "Ask somebody else." In the end, if thinking was easy, there would be more of it.

The fundamental difference between Mr. Prosser and Mr. Basil comes down to who is finally responsible for learning. Mr. Prosser's approach implies that the teacher is, while Mr. Basil's suggests that students' should be. Can anyone convince students they are responsible for their own learning other than students themselves? And isn't it usually through discussion, dialogue, and problem solving—not through lecture—that students come to realize what they *have*, and *have not* learned?

Not long ago, I heard James Howard of the Council for Basic Education state on National Public Radio, "Education is what you have left after you have forgotten everything you learned in school." I wonder what Mr. Prosser would make of that statement. I know what Mr. Basil would do with it.

(*Note:* An edited version of this article, "Hail, Socrates," appeared in *Teacher* magazine (May-June, 1999, pp. 62–63).)

Figure 1.1 compares and contrasts important differences between the two models of teaching discussed in this article.

FIGURE 1.1 TWO MODELS OF TEACHING AND LEARNING

Didactic	*Socratic*
Passive Learning [*Master/Disciple*]	**Active Learning** [*Engaged inquiry*]
1. Teacher centered: based on the assumption that the teacher is the primary agent in learning.	1. Problem centered: based on the assumption that the student is the primary agent in learning.
2. Teacher's role: to impart the results of experience, personal study, and reflection.	2. Teacher's role: to uncover the question that the answer hides. To be a colearner.
3. Primarily deductive: the usual methods are lecture, story telling, and use of analogy.	3. Primarily inductive: the usual methods are discussion, dialogue, and problem solving.
4. Test of truth: authority and/or experience.	4. Test of truth: reason and evidence.
5. Learning is the reception of ideas.	5. Learning is a conflict of ideas: a thesis, an antithesis, and a synthesis that results in new knowledge (Hegel).
6. Student's role: to be passive, open, receptive, trusting, and unquestioning.	6. Student's role: to be active, questioning, critical, and discriminating—to learn to trust one's own judgment (independent thinking).
7. Evaluation is factual recall of data—form of objective tests and right and wrong answers.	7. Evaluation is application of understanding and interpretation of data—commonly in an essay.
8. Ultimate goal: wisdom viewed as an internalization of truths and beliefs.	8. Ultimate goal: wisdom viewed as an informed ignorance—knowing what one does not know, the Socratic paradox.

AFTERWORD

"The school that fails to teach thinking fails in everything."

Richard Mitchell,
Less Than Words Can Say

While Chapter 1 illustrates the importance of the Socratic method for active learning, the didactic model still has a necessary but minor role since teachers sometimes must also provide organized information not accessible other ways. The two generic lesson plans, compared and contrasted in Figure 1.2, reveals important differences.

WHAT'S NEXT: AN OVERVIEW OF THIS BOOK

Having illustrated crucial differences between a Socratic and lecturing teacher in the classroom, Chapter 2 asks you to reflect on a series of *seminal quotations* from master teachers who range from Alfred North Whitehead to school-reformer Theodore Sizer. Each author makes clear the basic differences between *passive* teaching and learning (didactic, infusion, lecture, or direct teaching) and *active* teaching and learning (Socratic, inductive, discovery, or problem-centered).

Chapter 3 is a complete, detailed, and illustrated explanation of our conception of the *Socratic method.* Chapter 4 focuses on preparing students to participate in text-based *Socratic seminars*, that is, discussions of a few representative short stories and novels. Although Stauffer's Directed Reading-Thinking Activity has been around a long time, it remains an important technique for a first reading of a story as a group activity. Chapter 5 presents guidelines and lesson plans for conducting Socratic discussions of the film versions of several short stories and plays often found in middle and high school curricula. Evaluation of each film takes the form of follow-up essays—comparison-contrast and persuasive. Finally, Chapter 6 is a full exposition of Literature Circles first developed by Harvey Daniels. While the topics follow closely the author's original conception of this kind of student-centered discussion, we have made important improvements in the role sheets and, most important, in helping students develop good prepared and spontaneous follow-up questions.

Finally, how do we know if students who engage in Socratic Seminars and Literature Circles are learning? Because standardized tests have taken on such importance as a means if not *the* means of assessment for some, we take up the all-important topic of assessment in Chapters 4 and 6.

FIGURE 1.2. LESSON PLAN MODELS

Didactic	*Socratic*
[Infusion]	[Discovery]
1. Focus: motivator.	1. Attention grabber, focus.
2. Objective: what students will be able to do by the end of the lesson.	2. Objective: to solve problems. What students may learn cannot be stated in advance.
3. Purpose: why lesson is important, useful, and relevant.	3. Purpose: to increase understanding and enjoyment of the group task and to develop the habit of independent and critical thinking.
4. Input: new information or activities.	4. Input: basic questions of interpretation and the coleaders' prepared and spontaneous follow-up questions.
5. Modeling: verbal or physical example of acceptable finished product or process.	5. Modeling: the coleaders follow the Four Rules of Socratic discussion.
6. Checking for understanding to determine if students have the information needed to complete the task.	6. Checking: coleaders ask follow-up questions for clarification, and substantiation, more opinion, consistency, implication, relevance, and resolution.
7. Guided practice: task done independently or in small groups with teacher assistance.	7. Guided practice: Students learn to rely on their own judgment about which answers are best and to distinguish the true from the false.
8. Closure: summary of should have been learned. The objective is restated or rephrased.	8. Closure: a written or oral resolution to the problem(s).

2

THEORY BEHIND THE SOCRATIC METHOD AND LITERATURE CIRCLES

Why is there such emphasis today on "engaged" learning, on "authentic" learning, and "active" learning? Are these adjectives today's new buzzwords for teaching and learning or are they old ideas that have been put into "new-and-improved" packaging? Today, parents, students, administrators, and teachers have become increasingly aware of the importance of active learning because passive learning too often results in no learning. Mel Silberman (*Active Learning: 101 Strategies*, 1996) and John Holt (*How Children Learn*, 1967) make clear the fundamental differences between passive (didactic, infusion, lecture, or "direct teaching") and active (inductive, discovery) teaching and learning.

DIFFERENCES BETWEEN PASSIVE AND ACTIVE LEARNING

Passive learning reveals several limitations:

- Student attention decreases with each passing minute.

- It appeals only to auditory learners and emphasizes memory.

- It tends to promote lower-level learning (factual content).

- It assumes that all students need the same information at the same time.

Active learning, in contrast, challenges students to:

- Learn how to state information in their own words.

- Illustrate ideas with their own examples.

- See connections between previous and present knowledge.

9

♦ Learn how to ask real questions (that have the element of doubt).

♦ Seek information to solve problems about meaning.

The seminal quotations in the section that follows clearly demonstrate that the contrast between active and passive learning is as old as the contrast between didactic (master-disciple) teaching and Socratic questioning (discovery learning). Are these two methods inherently irreconcilable, as some argue, or are they somehow complementary? More important, why do these master teachers emphasize the importance of active learning?

SEMINAL THOUGHTS FROM MASTER TEACHERS

♦ Alfred North Whitehead, *The Aims of Education* (1929, p. 38):

In training a child to activity of thought, above all things we must beware of 'inert ideas'—that is, ideas that are merely received into the mind without being utilized, or tested, or thrown into fresh combinations....Education with inert ideas is not only useless: it is above all things, harmful.

♦ Jacques Barzun, *Teacher in America*, "On Thinking" (1944, p. 72):

It is true that like all gifts of nature, the ability to think cannot be imparted; it can only be developed, and one of the oldest complaints against schools is that they turn the natural thinker into a learned dunce....Determined thinkers are few. For most people, thinking is dreary uphill work; their mind is set in motion by only a rare stimulus....Thinking is rare; that is one reason it is precious....Thinking means shuffling, relating, selecting the contents of one's mind so as to assimilate novelty, digest it, and create order. It is doing to a fact or an idea what we do to a beefsteak when we distribute its parts through our body....Discussion must not go off in all directions like a leaky hose. It must have a pattern, beginning at a given point and logically reaching another, from which to start again the next day....There must also be an atmosphere of freedom in which ideas are freely expressed and freely examined, sifted, rejected, and developed....Good discussion calls for the best teachers in their prime and I am convinced furthermore that it accomplishes more than any other form of teaching.

♦ Gilbert Highet, *The Art of Teaching* (1950, p. 151):

The tutorial method of teaching was invented by Socrates....He was the first who thought that teaching might mean, not pouring new ideas into an entirely empty brain, but drawing out universal truths from the mind in which they already lay concealed....For Socrates, teaching was not merely asking a series of questions, with the aim of exposing the pupil's ignorance or piercing his pretentions. These are negative ends. He had a positive end in view, although that end was concealed from the pupil. He wanted to make every pupil realize that truth was in the pupil's own power to find, if he searched long enough and hard enough, refusing all "authoritative statements" and judged every solution by reason alone....This system is the most difficult, the least common, and yet the most thorough way to teach—it is the right combination of critical method and positive purpose."

♦ Jerome S. Bruner, *Process of Education,* "Motives for Learning." (1960, pp. 72–73):

The issue [of motives for learning] is particularly relevant in an entertainment-orientated, mass-communication culture where passivity and "spectatorship" are dangers...active learning is the antithesis of the spectator's passivity....How, within this context, do we arouse the child's interest in the world of ideas?....*The principal recommendation is to increase the inherent interest of materials taught, giving the student a sense of discovery.*

♦ John Holt, *How Children Fail,* "Answer Grabbers or Problem Solvers?" (1964, p. 310):

We encourage children to act stupidly by boring them, by filling up their days with dull repetitive tasks that make little or no claim to their attention or demands on their intelligence....As a result, most children in school are answer-centered rather than problem-centered....They see a problem as a kind of announcement that, far off in some mysterious Answer land, there is an answer, which they are supposed to go out and find....When we give children answers, we call this "helping them."

♦ Northrup Frey, *The Educated Imagination* (1970, p. 39):

Thinking is an acquired habit founded on practice, like playing the piano. How well we do it depends on how much of it we have done, and it is never autonomous. We do not start to think about a subject:

we enter into a body of thought and try to add to it. It is only out of long discipline in continuous and structured thinking, whether in a school, in a profession, or in the experience of life, that any genuine wisdom can emerge.

♦ Mortimer J. Adler, *Reforming Education: The Opening to the American Mind* (1977, p. 290):

The ideal Socratic seminar occurs when the teacher is able to resort only to interrogative speech—when there is no declarative, but only interrogative teacher-talk, only the asking of questions....The more the seminar is an experience of active learning for the students, the sooner they will active learners in their reading of texts for future seminars and the sooner they will be able to engage in learning by themselves without the help of teachers, which is the ultimate desideratum of all teaching.

♦ Eleanor Kutz and Hephzibah Roskelly, *An Unquiet Pedagogy*, "The Student as Active Learner" (1991, p. 365):

Coming to know is an active process, in which the learner must be engaged in acts of discovery and inquiry; this process always takes place in interaction with others, but most classrooms isolate learners from that kind of interaction. The group in the classroom mirrors the way most people learn outside the classroom.....While teachers can establish activities that actively engage students as individuals in their learning...we argue that knowledge, because it is fundamentally shared and social, is fully created and negotiated only in collaborative contexts. So, while helping students become active learners and assume authority for their own learning, teachers must also create opportunities for them to share in knowing and coming to know."

♦ Harvery Daniels, *Literature Circles: Voice and Choice in the Student-Centered Classroom* (1994, pp. 23–24):

In literature circles, we *require* that students find and develop their own topics for discussion...if kids never practice digging the big ideas out of texts themselves and always have teachers doing it for them, how can they ever achieve literacy and intellectual independence?....The distinctive value of literature circles is that it enacts another paradigm of learning. It is based on a faith in self-directed practice. Literature circles embody the idea that kids learn to read mainly by reading and to write by writing and by doing so in a supportive, literate community.

♦ Mel Silberman, *Active Learning: 101 Strategies to Teach Any Subject* (1996, p. 10):

When learning is PASSIVE, the learner comes to the encounter without curiosity, without questions, and without interest in the outcome (except, perhaps, in the grade he or she will receive.) When learning is ACTIVE, the learner is seeking something. He or she wants an answer to a question, needs information to solve a problem, or is searching for a way to do a job.

♦ Theodore R. Sizer, *Horace's Hope: What Works for The American High School*, "What Matters" (1996, p. 189):

Good schools promote the habit of respectful skepticism—respectful in the sense that it rests on evidence and carefully established argument but is ever asking questions such as "Just why might this be so?" and "Is there another way of explaining this situation?" All humans revel in this process of inquiry to some extent. Asking questions captures our minds more readily than memorizing somebody else's answers to yet somebody else's questions. Good schools surely push forward the best of what disciplined minds in the past have sent down to us, but always by displaying yesterday's conclusions fundamentally as questions that always need fresh answers.

♦ Neil Postman and Charles Weingartner, *Linguistics: A Revolution in Education* (1997, p. 70):

What students most need to learn in schools is how to learn. This is the position taken by almost all modern educational philosophers, from John Dewey to Jerome Bruner....The emphasis is on the *how* of learning rather than the *what*....What is important is not that students be given answers—even "right" answers—but that they learn how answers are produced, how knowledge is generated, how learning is conducted....This view places subject matter, or content, in its proper perspective. Most people recognize that the schools have traditionally regarded the accumulation of facts as a wholly worthwhile goal in itself. But this is an odd anti-intellectualism that says to a student: You do not need to know how knowledge is generated—what skills, attitudes, and methods are needed in order to produce knowledge. You only need to memorize what others have already discovered through *their* inquiries....The inductive or discovery method of teaching, by stressing the procedure of inquiry—methods of evaluating as well as of gathering facts—attempts to develop in students a critical attitude toward authority [a textbook] and its pronouncements.

♦ J. Lloyd Trump, *Focus on Change: Guide to Better Schools* (1998, p. 179):

*Students need opportunities to develop the inquiring mind....*As they go through school, they should learn to react critically to what they read and hear and to approach problems with the curiosity, the will, and the techniques to solve them. *Students need to learn the skills of effective discussion.* More opportunities are needed for them to examine together issues within a subject area. Such examinations lead to critical thinking and stimulate further inquiry. Discussion in today's schools is too often limited to a few remarks between the teacher and a few pupils willing to speak....It is not merely useless but actually harmful to transmit the findings of any subject area *without providing at the same time* an understanding of the strategies of inquiry through which the findings were discovered. The disguised-lecture-method of discussion must be replaced with authentic inquiry in today's schools."

In the chapters that follow, we will do our best to bring the seminal thoughts to life in the classroom by explaining the Socratic method and providing practical exercises.

3

THE SOCRATIC METHOD OF TEACHING

OVERVIEW OF
THE SOCRATIC METHOD OF TEACHING
THE SOCRATIC PARADOX

*"The role of the teacher is to uncover the question
that the answer hides."*

James Baldwin

Let us begin at the source. Like so many students before him and even those today, Socrates' student Meno is exasperated by his teacher's refusal to "just tell him" what to do, what truth is, and in their dialogue, whether or not virtue can be taught. Meno is astounded when Socrates openly admits not only that he does not know whether virtue can be taught but also that he does not even know what virtue is. "What!" Meno asks: "Is this the report we are to take home about you?" In characteristic manner, Socrates challenges his student to re-phrase the question, to reflect on it, and to arrive at his own answer. In so doing, Socrates helps Meno wrestle with the implications of the problem that he has posed for their discussion. Indeed, Socrates makes a point of asserting his own ignorance: "All I can say is that I have often looked to see if there are any [teach-ers of virtue], and in spite of all my efforts, I cannot find them…I do not know what virtue is and, not only that, you may say also, that to the best of my belief, I have never yet met anyone who did know" (Rouse 29). Meno leaves con-founded that his teacher, his master and guide, refuses to confirm what Meno believes he already knows.

Nevertheless, as Socrates' reputation for wisdom continues to grow, another impetuous student, Chaerephon, goes to the oracle of Delphi to ask if anyone is wiser than Socrates. The priestess of Apollo, Pythia, replies that no one is. When Socrates hears the answer he is genuinely puzzled: "I have no wisdom, small or great. What can he mean when he says that I am the wisest of men?" (426). But why does Socrates take the oracle's word at face value? Could the god also have meant that no one was wiser than Socrates because wisdom is not to be found among men? Socrates is even more explicit about his ignorance in the defense of his life at his trial, *The Apology*. After questioning another who claimed to be wise, Socrates concludes, "I am better off than he is—for he knows nothing, and thinks that he knows; I neither know nor think that I know. In this latter particular, then, I seem to have the slight advantage over him" (327). What we have here is the great paradox of learning: we must first know what we want to know or recognize what we do not know. Is this confusing? Only at first. What Socrates suggests is that the first step to learning is knowing how to ask an honest question—one that you have no answer to or one that you have several answers to but none entirely satisfy. In short, unless you have questions, you cannot learn. As learning begins, the more you know, the more you [realize that] do not know. Such is the Socratic paradox.

THE SOCRATIC METHOD

But what about the Socratic method? The phrase is as elusive as a greased pig. What does the Socratic method mean to the teacher in the trenches? For some, unfortunately, it means no more than asking a lot of questions—rapidly and indiscriminately. For others, it means conducting an interview. And for still others it means cross-examination. A few even seem to believe that there is something mystical about the Socratic method—that some teachers are born with it or that there really is no method that teachers can acquire. Nevertheless, these notions miss the mark because they fail to capture the Socratic concept of teaching *and* do not recognize that the Socratic method can be explained, applied, and evaluated. Furthermore there is no "official" Socratic method since even today there is no consensus about Socrates' method as recorded in the dialogues of his most brilliant student, Plato. Nevertheless, I am bold enough to assert my own conception of a Socratic method in the following exposition.

♦ What is the Socratic method?

It is an exercise in "reflective thinking" that, according to John Dewey has two elements: *doubt*—a problem about meaning that initiates it—and *an act searching* for a solution(s) to solve that problem.

♦ How is it done?

It is conducted mainly by asking *prepared questions* (the problems that are the focus of discussion) and *spontaneous follow-up questions,* which develop the ideas being considered with a view to achieving resolution.

♦ *Why is it done this way?*

It is done this way to achieve the goal or purpose of this kind of engaged learning: to increase the groups' *and* the coleaders' understanding (comprehension) of the text under discussion. As a result, there will be an increase in enjoyment—that is, the satisfaction of discovering one's own answers and finding new meaning(s) in the selection.

In sum, the Socratic method begins with a *problem* (a prepared interpretive question), continues as a *process* of asking spontaneous follow-up questions, and results in a *product*—increased understanding and enjoyment.

TECHNIQUES OF ACTIVE AND CLOSE READING

"The person who does not spend at least as much time in actively and definitely thinking about what he has read as he has spent in reading, is simply insulting the author."

Arnold Bennett

A first step for participating in the Socratic Seminar is reading the selection. Far too many students read neither actively nor closely—not only because they have not learned how to discriminate among the various purposes of different kinds of reading but also because they have not been taught how to read actively. Here is an effective method if employed continually by teacher and student.

The phrase "active and close reading" suggests immediately two ideas. First, some books and stories deserve to be read closely, slowly, or actively—not only because we would miss many of their implied meanings but also because we must learn to recognize meanings other than our own in what we peruse. Second, there are times when how fast we read or how much we read is of no importance. What IS important is that we learn *to reflect* on what we read and learn how to carry on a conversation with the author. We converse with an author when we question always what he or she says.

The purpose of active and close reading is to learn to read interpretively—to pay attention not merely to WHAT an author says but to WHY he says it in the WAY that he does. In short, the purpose in reading imaginative literature (fiction) is not merely trying to recall what happens in a story, for example, but to think about why things happen as they do. With nonfiction, we have to take particular note of an author's choice of words (diction), use of sentence structure (syntax), and organization of ideas.

Some books and stories like those that we will be reading can be *interpreted in several ways*. And no individual, adult or child, teacher, or student, ever thinks of ALL possible interpretations in a given story. As a result, no one can tell you what is *the* correct interpretation of a story, poem, or play—not even, believe it or not, not even the author! However, this does *not* mean that all interpretations are equally good or correct. On the contrary, some interpretations are better than others and some are wrong. How can this be so? The answer is that some interpretations have more evidence to support them which makes them more plausible. And other interpretations are more comprehensive, that is, they explain more of a story than do other views. Still other interpretations are wrong: either there is no evidence to support them or the evidence offered is contradicted by some other statement of the author. But what about the author? Why doesn't he or she have the last word about what was "really meant"? Thomas Mann, in the extraordinary afterword of his novel, "The Making of *The Magic Mountain*,"says:

> I consider it a mistake to think that the author himself is the best judge of his work. He may be that while he is still at work on it and living in it. But once done, it tends to be something he has got rid of, something foreign to him; others, as time goes on, will know more and better about it than he. They can often remind him of things in it he has forgotten or indeed never quite knew.

Just as no one can tell you what is *the* correct interpretation nor what your interpretation must be, so also no one can tell you what details in your reading are important. Meaning can begin anywhere—even with what someone else might regard an insignificant detail. Whatever furnishes you with clues for arriving at your own interpretation, that is what is important. In short, what is important varies from reader to reader.

In addition, to interpret a work for yourself does *not* require that we first read about the author's life, or about the times in which the author lived, nor review general introductory statements. Instead, a reader can begin by noting his or her responses to a story and then try to convert as many of them as possible into questions. But to engage in this process fruitfully, a reader must learn to respect his or her own responses—that is, to take seriously personal thoughts and feelings about a book.

Forming good questions whose answers can yield a great deal of meaning about a story requires at least *two readings*. Roland Barthes, the eminent French literary critic, maintains that "He who reads a story only once is condemned to read the same story his whole life." On the *first reading*, the reader's main interest should be to note his responses in writing, that is, to make notations. Tom

Romano, a New York high school English teacher, says that "Reading without writing [here, notations] is like cooking without eating." During the *second reading*, note new responses and pay special attention to those notations that could be converted into questions.

Unless readers learn to put responses into writing by making notations as they read, they will have few questions—or, if there are any questions at all, they will be so general that they could be asked of any story. Such generic questions yield little new knowledge and yet without questions, no one can increase an understanding of the material. The first step to learning then, paradoxically, is knowing what you want to know—that is, asking a real question.

American educator and philosopher, Mortimer Adler, explains in his classic essay on "How to Mark a Book," that a notation is any response to the text that a reader puts into writing. Notations take various forms: underlining what is important, circling key words, drawing lines to make connections between similar parts, comments, personal, emotional reactions, reminders, and even nascent questions. As John Ruskin so aptly remarked, "No book is worth anything which is not worth much; nor is it serviceable until it has been read and reread, and loved, and loved again, *and marked*."

Experienced readers have found that whenever they mark up a text, they usually refer to one or more of these four sources for formulating questions:

1. *Whatever they think is important* (for whatever reason).

2. *Whatever they don't understand.* Not understanding something is more than circling unfamiliar vocabulary (although it includes this). It includes notations about a character's motivation, for example, or why the story begins or ends as it does, or what the author means by a certain statement or includes a certain scene, and so on.

3. *Whatever they like or dislike, agree or disagree with.* In other words, active readers are also careful to note their emotional responses.

4. *Whatever they think is related—one part of the text to another.* A chief concern of the second reading is looking for connections or patterns among various parts of the reading. For example:

   • The repetition of the same word or phrase.

   • The reoccurrence of similar actions.

   • Contrasting words or actions.

   • The place of something in the text (organization).

As with so many things in life, whatever we get out of something is proportionate to the effort we put into it. So too with reading. Unless we learn how to become thoughtful, active, and close readers, we will continue to miss many of the implications of what we read and, as a result, lose the pleasure of increasing our understanding of what we are reading.

Consider the notations that I have made on a well-known poem (Figure 3.1) that illustrate the different kinds of notations (Figures 3.2 (p. 22) and 3.3 (p. 23)). On the second reading, notice which of these responses were converted into discussion questions (Figure 3.4, p. 24).

THREE KINDS OF QUESTIONS

What does it say? What does it mean? Is it true?

Mortimer Adler

When did you first realize the importance of the kinds of questions you ask your students? Was it when you were puzzled about why some questions fell flat while others provoked immediate response? Was it when you suddenly realized your questions were not clear? Was it when you knew that you placed too much emphasis on factual or memory questions? Was it when you got into "bull sessions" as a result of emphasizing evaluative questions? Whatever the moment, few teachers would deny the importance of writing and asking good questions. On the other hand, my experience has been that while teachers recognize that questioning is an art, they are too often at a loss not only about how to write good discussion questions but also about how to sustain them in discussion.

Mortimer Adler, the eminent American philosopher and education reform leader, first formulated the three kinds of questions in 1948 in *A Guide for Leaders of Great Books Discussion Groups*. He asked: "What does the author say? What does the author mean? Is it true? *Fact, Interpretation, Evaluation*—these are the three levels of questions"(8). In 1956, Benjamin Bloom edited a *Taxonomy of Educational Objectives: Cognitive Domain*, which classified eight educational objectives that used examples of questions for each kind of thinking: knowledge (memory), comprehension, translation, interpretation, application, analysis, synthesis, and evaluation. Ten years later, Norris Sanders popularized Bloom's taxonomy for social studies teachers in his useful illustrations in his *Classroom Questions: What Kinds?*

Text continues on page 25.

FIGURE 3.1 *THE ROAD NOT TAKEN* BY ROBERT FROST

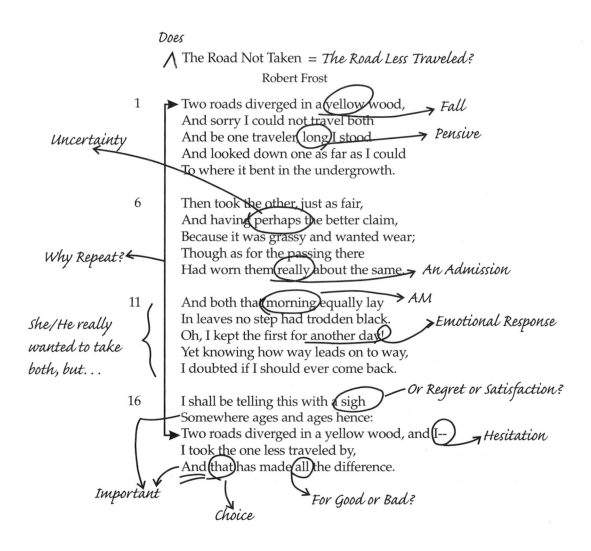

FIGURE 3.2 *THE ROAD NOT TAKEN*: FIRST READING

---

1. Whatever you think important:

    The speaker really would like to have taken both roads. (line 3)

    The speaker admits the two roads were really about the same. (10)

    He is taking about a major decision. (16)

2. Whatever you don't understand.

    Why isn't the title about the road less traveled?

    Why will the speaker be telling about his decision with a sigh?

3. Whatever you like or dislike, agree or disagree with.

    Whenever I make a choice, I too sometimes wonder what would have happened if I had chosen differently.

4. Whatever you think is related:

    - The repetition of the same word or phrase: First and seventeenth line.

    - The reoccurrence of similar actions: Choosing to look back on a previous choice.

    - Contrasting words or actions: Speaking about a choice and making that choice.

    - The place of something in the text (organization): Which word(s) of the last line need emphasis?

FIGURE 3.3 *THE ROAD NOT TAKEN*: SECOND READING—
NOTATIONS CONVERTED INTO QUESTIONS

---

1. Why is the title of the poem about the road *not* taken?

2. Why is the choice of the less traveled road made on a fall morning? (1,11)

3. Why would the speaker like to have taken both roads? (2, 13)

4. Why does the speaker say one road had "perhaps" the better claim? (7)

5. Why does the speaker admit both roads were about the same? (10)

6. Why is there an exclamation point at the end of line 13?

7. Is the sigh one of satisfaction or regret? (16)

8. Will the speaker be telling of his choice to others to only to himself? (16)

9. Why will the speaker be telling about his decision in future "ages"? (17)

10. Why does line 18 end with a dash?

11. Has the choice of the less traveled road been for the better or the worse?

FIGURE 3.4 ACTIVE AND CLOSE READING

The purpose of active and close reading is to learn to read *interpretively*—to pay attention not merely to *what* an author says but to *why* the author says it in the *way* that he or she does. In short, the purpose in reading imaginative literature (fiction) is not merely trying to recall what happens in a story but to think about why things happen as they do. With nonfiction, we have to take particular note of an author's choice of words (diction), use of sentence structure (syntax), and the organization of ideas.

Active reading requires a minimum of *two readings*. The purpose of the first reading is to note your responses in writing by making notations. During the second reading note new responses and pay special attention to those notations that could be converted into questions.

Experienced readers have found that whenever they mark up a text, they usually mark one or all of these *four sources* for formulating questions:

1. *Whatever they think is important* (for whatever reason).

2. *Whatever they don't understand.* Not understanding something is more than circling unfamiliar vocabulary (although it includes this). It includes notations about a character's motivation, for example, or why the story begins or ends as it does, or what the author means by a certain statement or includes a certain scene, and so on.

3. *Whatever they like or dislike, agree, or disagree with.* In other words, active readers are also careful to note their emotional responses.

4. *Whatever they think is related*—one part of the text to another. A chief concern of the second reading is looking for connections or patterns among various parts of the reading. For example:

   • The repetition of the same word or phrase.

   • The recurrence of similar actions.

   • Contrasting words or actions.

   • The place of something in the text (organization).

But do teachers need eight kinds of questions? Not in my experience. Too often have I been in workshops where teachers get into vigorous and pointless arguments about identifying types of questions. Bloom's and Sanders' works have value for developing standardized tests, but for classroom discussion their added distinctions are not needed since it becomes evident in discussion that translation, application, analysis, and synthesis can be put under the umbrella of interpretation. Knowledge or memory questions are factual, and evaluation is about personal values or experience. In other words, classroom teachers do well enough, as do most of our colleagues, to recognize the vital difference between *the purpose* of each type of question: To check for recall (factual)? To check for understanding (interpretation)? or, To check for personal relevance and application (evaluation)?

Here is how I explain and illustrate the three kinds of questions for my students. After reading and reviewing notations on *The Road Not Taken*, I check for their understanding of these different types of questions with a bonus practice quiz (see handouts). I want to add that teaching students how to recognize and write their own interpretive questions can increase significantly their understanding of the reading even *without discussion*.

THE ROAD NOT TAKEN
LESSON PLAN 1:
THREE KINDS OF QUESTIONS

1. Focus:

   What questions do you have about this object (choose something not easily recognizable) in my hand? List briefly on overhead or blackboard.

2. Objective:

   To understand by identifying the three types of questions that can be asked about a reading.

3. Purpose:

   Why are the three types of questions important? To be able to write your own questions. To increase your understanding (comprehension) of the reading by writing interpretive questions. To understand the purpose of each of the three basic kinds of questions.

4. Input and modeling:

   Review handout on the three kinds of questions. Complete with examples on overhead. Have students copy examples on their handouts.

5. Checking:

   Review definitions of the three types of questions. Review directions for practice exercise.

6. Guided practice:

   Review quiz with entire class. Peer grading. Bonus points.

7. Closure:

   Return to questions that students asked about the object in your hand at beginning of class. Point out which questions had only one answer (fact), could be answered in more than one way based on the evidence (interpretation), and those that were about evaluation (experience or values).

Note: This lesson is set up for a 50-minute period. If you have a 90-minute period in a block schedule, you could extend the guided practice by having pairs write sequences of related questions (see examples). Another option: have groups of 4 write 10 interpretive questions on the next reading.

THREE KINDS OF QUESTIONS

1. *Factual:* A factual question has only one correct answer. It asks the reader to recall something that the author said or to read a passage from the text where an answer can be found. Its answer depends more on memory than thinking.

    Example: *At what time of day did the poet choose the less traveled road?*

    Note: Sometimes a factual question does require some thinking to answer correctly but it is still factual because only one answer is possible based on a careful reading of the text.

    Example: *At what time of year did the poem choose the less traveled road?* Answer: yellow wood means that it was fall.

2. *Interpretation:* An interpretive question has more than one correct answer because a difference of opinion about meaning is possible. It asks the reader to explain *what the author means by what is said*. The answer depends more on thinking than on memory or recall.

    Example: *Has the choice of the less traveled road been for better or worse?*

3. *Evaluation:* An evaluative question asks you to think about your own values or experiences. Such questions sometimes ask a reader to consider how he or she would act in a situation similar to one a character in the story finds himself of if he or she has had a similar experience.

    Example: (common experience) *What was one of the most important choices that you have made in your life?*

    Example: (values) *Do you agree that important, life-changing choices should not be made without getting advice from others?*

    Note: The *test* for distinguishing between the three types of questions is to begin answering the question itself for a half minute. If you begin talking about the text, the question is factual *or* interpretive. If it has only one answer, it is factual; if it can be answered in more than one way, *if you have to explain your answer,* it is interpretive. In contrast, if you begin to talk about your own experiences or values, if you go outside the text, it is a question of evaluation.

THREE KINDS OF QUESTIONS:
THE ROAD NOT TAKEN—PRACTICE QUIZ

Directions: First, answer each question briefly in the space beneath it. Second, at the left, label the type of question as *Fact* for factual, *Int* for interpretation, and *Eval* for evaluation.

_____   1. Would the poet like to have taken both roads?

_____   2. Why will the poet be telling about his decision in the distant future?

_____   3. Whenever you have to make an important decision, do you sometimes regret not being able to make another choice?

_____   4. Does the sigh in line 16 suggest satisfaction or regret?

_____   5. Will the speaker be telling of his choice to others or only to himself?

_____   6. Why does line 18 end with a dash?

_____   7. Have you made any choices in your life that you believe the majority of your friends have not made?

_____   8. Why does the last stanza of the poem echo the first stanza?

_____   9. Why does the poet wish that he could have taken both roads?

_____   10. Looking back, is the poet trying to convince himself that he has made the better choice of the less traveled road?

Three Kinds of Questions:
The Road Not Taken—Answer Key

Directions: First, answer each question briefly in the space beneath it. Second, at the left, label the type of question as *Fact* for factual, *Int* for interpretation, and *Eval* for evaluation.

_____ 1. Would the poet like to have taken both roads?
Factual: Yes. In line two, he says he is sorry he could not travel both.

_____ 2. Why will the poet be telling about his decision in the distant future?
Interpretation: He knows that he is making an important choice that he will be speaking about with pride and satisfaction. He may also be fearful that his choice may not have been the best. Other answers are possible.

_____ 3. Whenever you have to make an important decision, do you sometimes regret not being able to make another choice?
This is an **evaluation** question about personal experience.

_____ 4. Does the sigh in line 16 suggest satisfaction or regret?
Interpretation: Several lines in the poem make either answer plausible.

_____ 5. In the future, how will the poet be telling of his choice.
Factual: He says that he will be speaking with a sigh. (line 16)

_____ 6. Why does line 18 end with a dash?
Interpretation: The dash could suggest hesitation about the worth of his choice. It may also suggest that he is recalling with pride that he made the best choice. Other answers are also possible.

_____ 7. Have you made any choices in your life that you believe the majority of your friends have not made?
This is an **evaluation** question about personal values.

_____ 8. When does the poet make his choice of the less traveled road?
Factual: He makes his choice on a fall morning. (lines 1 and 11)

_____ 9. Does the poet look down both roads as far as he could?
Factual: No. He says he looked as far as he could down the road that he did not take and then took the other. (lines 4–6)

_____ 10. Looking back, is the poet trying to convince himself that he has made the better choice of the less traveled road?
Interpretation: Several lines indicate that he may be rationalizing a decision made long ago. On the other hand, he may be simply patting himself on the back that he made the best choice and has no regrets.

Here is a useful exercise that gives you further practice in testing your own and the group's understanding of the differences between the three kinds of questions.

AN EXERCISE ON WRITING
SEQUENCES OF RELATED QUESTIONS

Directions: With your coleader, write 10 interpretive questions on the reading with a line reference for each. Select your two best questions and then write a related question of fact and evaluation for each. Begin with a factual question. For example:

Factual: Does the speaker of the poem hesitate before he took the less-traveled road?

Interpretation: Why does the speaker stand for a long time before choosing the road less-traveled?

Evaluation: At what times in your life did you hesitate before you decided to do something?

QUALITIES OF GOOD PREPARED
DISCUSSION QUESTIONS

"What are you asking me, Mr. M—?"

As a teacher you must have been puzzled about why some questions in class fall flat when others evoke immediate response. While student inattention and unwillingness to think may explain some of the lack of response, we must also look at the quality of the questions that we ask. Some questions are so general or unclear that no one could hope for a reasonable response. In short, those questions that evoke next to no response may lack one of the important qualities of good prepared discussion questions whereas those that generate ideas for discussion may have all the necessary qualities. Here's how we explain and illustrate the six characteristics of good discussion questions. A good prepared question should be:

- ◆ *Clear:* A clear question says what it means so that no one has to guess what the questioner has in mind. A question that is not clear is like asking someone to find something but not telling him or her what to look for. If the question has to be explained or if it cannot be rephrased, it is not clear. In short, the effort in discussion should be expended on trying to solve the problem, not in trying to figure out the question!

♦ *Interpretative:* Becaused the primary aim of shared inquiry is to increase your own and the group's understanding of the reading, center on questions of interpretation. In addition, factual questions do not generate discussion since they have but one correct answer. Furthermore, when questions of evaluation become the focus of discussion, too often discussion becomes a bull session.

♦ *Specific:* A good discussion question must be specific or tailor-made to the reading so that it could be asked only of one text and not of another. This is not a matter of being picky or merely naming a character *but a matter of being precise, that is, of pinpointing a problem.*

♦ *Doubt:* There must be doubt in the mind of the person who formulated the question for it to function in discussion. Without the vital element of doubt about the answer to the question, there can be no increased understanding or insight. A question has the element of doubt *either* when the questioner can think of no answer at all *or*, as is the case more often, when the questioner can think of more than one answer but none are fully satisfactory. In this case doubt is a matter of degree; it is not complete. *This characteristic of a good prepared question is what makes the concept of the Socratic method presented here unique.* It is its distinguishing mark.

♦ *Answerable on the basis of the text alone.* Avoid questions that go outside the text and ask a reader to offer a speculative answer, that is, one that cannot be supported one way or another from the text itself. Such questions are unsatisfying because with them, one answer sounds as good as another. Caveat: do not confuse a question that has complete doubt with one that is unanswerable. In other words, do not quickly dismiss a question as unanswerable merely because, at the moment, you can think of no answer to it.

♦ *Care or concern* about the answer. Ask questions that interest you personally *not* what you think might interest someone else. This personal quality adds intensity to a discussion that is lost without it.

THE ROAD NOT TAKEN
LESSON PLAN 2:
QUALITIES OF GOOD
DISCUSSION QUESTIONS

1. Focus:	What are the characteristics of a good discussion question?
2. Objective (what):	To identify and illustrate the six qualities of good discussion questions.
3. Purpose (why):	To write your own questions for discussion that increase our understanding and enjoyment of the reading. To carry on a conversation with the author while reading.
4. Input and Modeling:	Review first the checklist on the qualities of good discussion questions (handout).
5. Checking:	Review directions for the practice exercise (handout).
6. Guided Practice:	Review the quiz with the entire class. Peer grading. Bonus points.
7. Closure:	What kind of question generates a lively discussion? Review briefly the six qualities of good questions.

Note: This lesson plan is set up for a 50-minute period. If you have a 90-minute period in a block schedule, you could extend the guided practice by having students apply the checklist to the ten questions that they wrote for the first reading. Another option would be to explain and illustrate the three levels of doubt in good questions.

QUALITIES OF GOOD DISCUSSION QUESTIONS: CHECKLIST FOR EVALUATING QUESTIONS

Any question that generates a lively discussion has several characteristics. Is it clear, specific, and interpretive. It also has the vital element of doubt about the answer but is answerable on basis of the story alone. Finally, it is a problem that the questioner cares about, that is, something that he or she really wants to solve. To avoid wasting discussion time, check your questions first to be sure that they have these six qualities. *In the order given,* use the questions on this checklist to evaluate your questions.

1. *Is my question clear?* Does my question make sense as written? Would I have to explain a word or phrase for someone who does not understand what I am getting at? If yes, mark your question NC for not clear and try to revise it if you can. If no, that is, if you think your question is clear, go on to the next step.

2. *Is my question specific?* Is my question so general that it could be asked of any story? Have I pinpointed a *problem* about meaning? If no, mark the question NS and try to revise it. If yes, that is, if your question can be asked only of this reading because it is tailor-made, go on to the next step.

3. *Is my question interpretive?* Have I written a factual question? If yes, mark NIF for not interpretive but factual and try to revise. Could I have written an evaluative question? If yes, mark NIE for not interpretive but evaluative and try to revise. However, if there is more than one answer to my question, that is, if someone could disagree based on their reading of the story, go on to next step.

4. *Does my question have the vital element of doubt about the answer?* Do I already have an answer in mind to this question? If yes, can I think of a second, equally plausible answer? If no, mark it LD for lacks doubt and try to revise by reviewing the three levels of doubt in writing interpretive questions. If you can think of no answer to your question, or if you can think of at least two equally good answers based on the text, go on to the next step.

5. *Is my question answerable on basis of the reading alone* or does it go outside the information given in the story? If no, mark UA for unanswerable and try to revise. Note: do not conclude that if you can think of no answer to your question, do not dismiss it immediately as unanswerable. You will learn in discussion whether or not it is answerable.

6. *Do I care about getting an answer* to this question in discussion? If no, mark LC for lacks care and write a question that really bothers you and you want to answer. If yes, mark your question GOOD because you know you have a written a question that will generate a lively discussion that will increase your own and the groups' understanding and enjoyment of the reading.

QUALITIES OF GOOD DISCUSSION QUESTIONS: THE ROAD NOT TAKEN—PRACTICE EXERCISE

Directions: Which of these questions would be suitable for discussion? At the left of each question, mark *Good* if it has the six qualities of good discussion questions. Mark *NC* if the question is not clear. Mark *NS* if the question is not specific and could be asked of any story with a minor word change. Mark *LD* for lacks doubt because it cannot be answered in more than one way. Mark *NI* for not interpretive because it is factual or evaluative. Mark *UA* for unanswerable on basis of the text alone.

_____   1.   What is the significance of the title?

_____   2.   Was it important to the poet to have taken the less traveled road?

_____   3.   Is Frost upset about arbitrary decisions?

_____   4.   Why is the title about the road not taken rather than about the road less traveled?

_____   5.   What is this poem all about?

_____   6.   What symbolic meanings can you find in the poem?

_____   7.   When was the last time you had a hard time making a decision?

_____   8.   Did the poet take time to think about which road to choose?

_____   9.   When did the poet really choose the less traveled road?

_____   10. Does the road less traveled stand for not getting married?

_____   11. Why does the poet wish that he could have taken both roads?

_____   12. Why did the poet decide to take the road less traveled?

_____   13. What is the big deal about using a road?

_____   14. Did the poet forget about the road that he didn't take?

_____   15. Does the last line of the poem refer to a good or bad difference?

QUALITIES OF GOOD DISCUSSION QUESTIONS: *THE ROAD NOT TAKEN*—ANSWER KEY

Directions: Which of these questions would be suitable for discussion? At the left of each question, mark *Good* if it has the six qualities of good discussion questions. Mark *NC* if the question is not clear. Mark *NS* if the question is not specific and could be asked of any story with a minor word change. Mark *LD* for lacks doubt because it cannot be answered in more than one way. Mark *NI* for not interpretive because it is factual or evaluative. Mark *UA* for unanswerable on basis of the text alone.

__NS__   1. What is the significance of the title?
          Not specific: can be asked of any title of any story or poem; it is not enough of a problem.

__LD__   2. Was it important to the poet to have taken the less traveled road?
          Lacks doubt: All the evidence points to yes; nothing supports no.

__NC__   3. Is Frost upset about arbitrary decisions?
          Not clear: "arbitrary decisions" needs clarification.

GOOD   4. Why is the title about the road not taken rather than about the road less traveled?
          Good question for discussion—a nice revision of the first question.

__NS__   5. What is this poem all about?
          Not specific: can be asked of any title of any story or poem.

__NS__   6. What symbolic meanings can you find in the poem?
          Not specific: can be asked of any title of any story or poem.

__NIE__ 7. When was the last time you had a hard time making a decision?
          Not interpretive but evaluation.

__NIF__ 8. Did the poet take time to think about which road to choose?
          Not interpretive but factual. (line 3)

__NC__   9. When did the poet really choose the less traveled road?
          Not clear: What does "really" mean?

__UA__ 10. Does the road less traveled stand for not getting married?
          Unanswerable on basis of the text alone.

GOOD 11. Why does the poet wish that he could have taken both roads?
          Good question for discussion—several answers are possible.

__NIF__ 12. Why did the poet decide to take the road less traveled?
          Not interpretive but factual. He gives three reasons. (lines 6–7)

__NC__ 13. What is the big deal about using a road?
          Not clear: what does the question mean?

__NIF__ 14. Did the poet forget about the road that he didn't take?
          Not interpretive but factual. He "kept it for another day." (line 13)

GOOD 15. Does the last line of the poem refer to a good or bad difference?
          Good question for discussion: either answer is possible.

THREE LEVELS OF DOUBT IN GOOD DISCUSSION QUESTIONS: *THE ROAD NOT TAKEN*

To avoid writing and asking questions that lack real doubt in the minds of the of the co-leaders, they must begin at their deepest level of perception or understanding of the text. To do so, they must sometimes write a question based on an assumption or even a hypothesis. In short, not all questions should be neutral or void of any previous understandings or interpretations. The following questions illustrate the three levels of doubt or degrees or perception.

1. *Neutral:* The leaders question the significance of a fact, a detail, an event, the choice of vocabulary, a sentence, or a phrase. [What is the meaning of X?]

   Examples:

   - Why is the title of the poem about the road not taken?
   - Why is there a pause at the end of line 18?
   - Why is the first line of the poem repeated in the last stanza?

2. *Assumption:* The leaders' question is based on a prior interpretation; the question is not neutral but based on a previous understanding. [Because X seems to be true, how do we explain Y?]

   Examples:

   - Why is the poem's speaker so pleased with his/her choice of the less-traveled road?
   - Why does the poet use the metaphor of a road to reflect on an important life decision?
   - Why is the poem's speaker uncertain that the road he/she chose had the better claim?

3. *Hypothesis:* The leader's question is a guess at meaning or an attempt to explain something in light of something else. The level of doubt here is in the *maybe—* what *may* be true. [Does X explain Y?]

   Examples:

   - Does the pause in line 18 suggest regret?
   - Can the title of the poem also refer to the road less traveled?
   - Has the choice of the less-traveled road been for better or worse?

   NOTE: It is important to distinguish questions based on assumptions or hypotheses from leading questions. Leading questions by definition lack doubt and indicate the answer expected. Leading questions always have tell-tale words or phrases in them: really, honestly, truly, or a negative. Leading questions never have a place in Socratic discussion.

   Examples:

   - Does the poet really think he/she has made the better choice?
   - Isn't it true that the poet is unhappy about choosing the less-traveled road?
   - How could any one honestly think that poet is unhappy with his/her choice of the less-traveled road?

ON WRITING BASIC
QUESTIONS OF INTERPRETATION

After you have conducted several discussions of interpretation, you will observe sooner or later that some interpretive questions require you to look at many lines and passages of a reading and give rise to a number of other related questions about the author's meaning. Those interpretive questions that consistently lead to sustained discussion (about 30 minutes per question) are *basic questions*. Consider the difference between these two questions on *The Road Not Taken*.

- ♦ Why will the speaker of the poem be telling about his decision in the future?

- ♦ Has the choice of the less-traveled road been for the better or the worse? Both questions are interpretive, but the first is fairly easy to resolve. You could probably find some satisfactory answer just by re-reading the last stanza. The speaker may be implying that he will be proud to tell someone about a choice he made when much younger. The sigh is one of satisfaction. On the other hand, since he would like to have taken both roads, he may be second-guessing himself or simply wondering if his life would have been any different had he taken the other road.

In contrast, to satisfactorily answer the second question, you would likely have to explore a number of related questions. For example: Why is the title of the poem about the road not taken? Why does the speaker wish that he could have taken both roads? Why does the speaker say the road less traveled had "perhaps" the better claim? Why does the speaker say he kept the choice of the first road for another day? Is the speaker trying to convince himself that he has made the better choice of the road less traveled? And so on. To answer these additional questions, and others you might think of that have something to do the value of the speaker's decision would take a great deal more time to answer than would the first question about why he is thinking about the far distant future. In short, the second question is *basic* because it deals with a major issue or problem in the poem that requires you to interpret a great deal of the text before you could answer it satisfactorily.

Centering discussion on basic questions has two advantages. First, they add a new dimension to thinking about interpretive questions because they require you to organize more facts and ideas to deepen your understanding of the poem. Second, basic questions yield a more comprehensive and integrated explanation of the author's meaning than you would have discussing interpretive questions that cover an assortment of unrelated topics or problems about meaning.

But how do you find and write basic questions for discussion? There are two methods:

♦ Begin by choosing any interpretive question that you care about and then try to write a number of interpretive questions that are related to it and help explore its implications; or,

♦ After you have written at least 20 interpretive questions on the reading, look for a pattern of common topics to which some of them seem to be related.

Whatever method you use, the goal is to formulate a *cluster* of related questions. Hence, a basic question is defined as *a cluster of at least eight related interpretive questions each one of which is a distinct problem for discussion*. In other words, each subquestion or follow-up question is an aspect or a piece of a comprehensive answer to the basic question. Like all interpretive questions these follow-up questions should have the qualities of any good discussion question.

In short, the basic question is the *problem* to be solved in discussion; the cluster is the coleaders' *plan* to solve it, and the reading selection is the source of information needed to resolve it.

The model basic question on Robert Frost's poem, illustrates the characteristics of good basic questions just described and explained. From this model and the foregoing discussion, we can identify four characteristics of a good basic question:

♦ All questions in the cluster are interpretive;

♦ All are related to the problem;

♦ None are repetitious; and,

♦ There are at least eight questions in the cluster.

According to Frost, has the speaker's choice of the less-traveled road been for the better or the worse?

♦ If it has been for the better, then:

• Why is the title of the poem about the road not taken?

• Why does the speaker wish that he could have taken both roads? (line 2)

• Why does the speaker say that the road less traveled had "perhaps" the better claim? (line 7)

• Why is there an exclamation point at the end of line 13?

- Why does the speaker say that he will be telling us about his choice of the less-traveled road with a sigh? (line 16)

- Does the final line of the poem refer to a good or bad difference?

♦ If it has been for the worse, then:

  - Does the title of the poem refer to the road less traveled or to the road that most people would have taken?

  - Why does the speaker admit, in retrospect, that both roads were really about the same? (line 10)

  - Why does the speaker say he kept the choice of the first road for another day? (line 13)

  - Why does the speaker say he will be telling about his decision "ages and ages hence"? (line 17)

  - Why is there a dash after "I" in line 18?

  - Is the speaker trying to convince himself that he has made the better choice in taking the road less traveled?

SPONTANEOUS FOLLOW-UP QUESTIONS

"The role of the teacher [leader] is to uncover the question that the answer hides."

James Baldwin

Why do some discussions fail even when you know that you began with a good interpretive question? Without doubt, such discussions so often fall flat, go nowhere, become chaotic, or degenerate into bull sessions because the leaders do not listen to what they hear. As a result, they miss opportunity after opportunity to follow-up on the ideas of the participants. A further consequence is that because answers are not developed, no one has any sense of satisfaction or gain in understanding.

The chief role of the coleaders in discussion is to direct traffic, that is, to direct and control the flow of ideas among the participants. Coleaders fulfill this role by introducing prepared questions to initiate discussion, basic or otherwise, and by asking spontaneous follow-up questions to develop and to connect ideas that help solve the problems under discussion. By following these guidelines, you lead an effective discussion that increases your own and the group's understanding of the reading. As a result, you also increase your mutual enjoyment of the reading, the ultimate goal of the Socratic seminar.

If you remember that there is no such thing as a perfect or ideal follow-up question, you will not make your role more difficult by trying to second-guess yourself. In other words, there several distinct kinds of follow-up questions that could be asked at any given moment of discussion. The kind of follow-up question asked in a specific situation depends on the leader's purpose.

- Is it *to clarify*? For example, "What did you mean when you said _____?" or "Could you explain more of what you mean by _____?"

- Is it *to substantiate*? For example, "Upon what in the reading are you basing your answer?" or "How do you know? What in the reading gave you that impression?"

- Is it *to get more opinion*? For example, "Maria, do you agree with John's view that _____? If so, could you explain? If not, why do you disagree?"

- Is it *to test for consistency*? For example, "Sarah, if what you say is correct, then how do you explain _____?"

- Is it *to relate* a response to the prepared question? For example, "Brian, how does what you have just said help answer our question about _____?"

- Is it *to draw out the implications* of a response? For example, "Ryan, are you saying _____?" "By _____ do you mean _____?"

- Or, finally, is it *to resolve* the prepared question. For example, "John, at this time what is your best answer to our question about _____? Or, "Laura, how many different answers have you heard to far to our basic question?"

How often must a leader make a choice about what to pursue, to table, or to ignore? Experience shows that the coleaders must ask an average of one follow-up question for every two or three responses. Unless the leaders maintain this average by asking enough follow-up questions, discussion soon reverts to a series of random, unrelated, off-the-cuff comments characteristic of mundane conversation.

The following practice exercise on follow-up questions (Lesson Plan 3) for "The Road Not Taken" will help you to understand and illustrate for your students the kinds and purposes of good follow-up questions. The purpose of these exercises is to help you and your students think about, before an actual discussion, how they (as coleaders) would deal with common situations, sometimes difficult, that often come up during discussion.

For example, what follow-up question could a leader ask when: (a) a single response contains multiple ideas; (b) the answer is evaluative, based on personal experience, not the text; (c) there is a failure to remember something in the reading; (d) there is no response at all or the participant ignores the question; (e) the answer is wrong; (f) the reply is undeveloped or not clear; (g) the participant does not understand the question; or, finally, (h) when several students respond in rapid fashion?

THE ROAD NOT TAKEN
LESSON PLAN 3:
SPONTANEOUS FOLLOW-UP QUESTIONS

1. Focus:	During discussion how can you tell if the coleaders are listening to your responses? They follow-up on your ideas with questions of clarification, substantiation, consistency, and so on.
2. Objective (what):	To prepare coleaders to ask good follow-up questions that are based on participant's responses. To learn how to develop participant's ideas in discussion. To anticipate some common problems that arise for coleaders during discussion.
3. Purpose (why):	To anticipate and learn how to handle some common problems that arise for coleaders during discussion.
4. Input:	Review exercise on spontaneous follow-up questions.
5. Modeling:	Review exercise on spontaneous follow-up questions.
6. Checking:	Review exercise with entire class.
7. Guided Practice:	Review exercise with entire class.
8. Closure:	Review the kind and purpose of the seven types of spontaneous follow-up questions.

SPONTANEOUS FOLLOW-UP QUESTIONS:
THE ROAD NOT TAKEN—PRACTICE EXERCISE

1. Leader: Why is the title of the poem about the road *not* taken?

   John: That is strange. After reading the poem, I expected the title to be "The Road Less Traveled," but it wasn't. Maybe he feels bad about not taking the first road. He did say that he wished he could have taken both roads.

   Follow-up
   question: _____

2. Leader: Why would the poet like to have taken both roads if he could have?

   Maria: Like anybody, he wants to have it both ways. Who wouldn't like to have it both ways?

   Follow-up
   question: _____

3. Leader: Why does the poet look down the road that he did not take rather than the one he finally decided on?

   Katie: He looked down the first road?

   Follow-up
   question: _____

4. Leader: Why does the poet say one road had "perhaps" the better claim but then admit that they were really about the same?

   Tony: I don't have a clue. Call on somebody else. Anyway, who cares?

   Follow-up
   question: _____

5. Leader: Why does Frost have the choice of the less-traveled road take place on a fall morning?

   Melissa: Fall? It wasn't during fall at all. He made his choice during summer.

   Follow-up
   question: _____

6. Leader: In line 16, is the sigh one of satisfaction or regret?

    Richard: Satisfaction, of course. That's what the poem is all about.

    Follow-up
    question: _____

7. Leader: Why will the poet be telling about his decision in the far distant future?

    Mary: Far-distant future? What are you talking about?

    Follow-up
    question: _____

8. Leader: Has the choice of the less traveled road been for better or worse?

    Buster: For sure it has been for the better. That is exactly why he says that he took the less-traveled road.

    Roger: It has to be for the worse because I think she is trying to talk herself into believing that she did not make a bad choice.

    Rita: Neither. I think the person is just saying that he or she made a choice and that was that.

    Follow-up
    question: _____

Note: See summary sheet on the nature and use of spontaneous follow-up questions.

SPONTANEOUS FOLLOW-UP QUESTIONS:
THE ROAD NOT TAKEN—ANSWER KEY

1. Leader: Why is the title of the poem about the road *not* taken?

   John: That is odd. After reading the poem, I expected the title to be "The Road Less Traveled," but it wasn't. Maybe he feels bad about not taking the first road. He did say that he wished he could have taken both roads.

   Comment: *How do you deal with several ideas in a response?* Follow-up on any one of them but do not ignore them all (except those clearly irrelevant) by merely asking for more opinion. For example, "John, why did you expect the title to be about the road less traveled?" (clarification) or, "John, what in the poem makes you think he might feel bad about not choosing the first road?" or, "John, why do you think he would have liked to have taken both roads?"

2. Leader: Why would the poet like to have taken both roads if he could have?

   Maria: Like anybody, he wants to have it both ways. Who wouldn't like to have it both ways?

   Follow-up
   question: _____

   Comment: *The answer is evaluative, based on personal experience, not the poem.* The solution is to turn Maria into the text. For example, "Maria, what in the poem (substantiation) makes you think the speaker wants it "both ways?" or, "Maria, what do you mean by having "it both ways"?"

3. Leader: Why does the poet look down the road that he did not take rather than the one he finally decided on?

   Katie: He looked down the first road?

   Follow-up
   question: _____

   Comment: *Here is a failure to remember something in the text.* Three options seem evident: (a) Ask Katie to look up the relevant line. (b) Ask someone else if he or she remembers his looking down the first road. (c) Rephrase the question with the relevant line in it. For example, "Katie, in line four , why does the speaker say he looked down the first road as far as he could?

4. Leader: Why does the poet say one road had "perhaps" the better claim but then admit that they were really about the same?

Tony: I don't have a clue. Call on somebody else. Anyway, who cares?

Follow-up
question: _____

Comment: *No response at all and a resistance to thinking* (which is not uncommon in early discussions). Six options suggest themselves: (a) Repeat the question to give the student time to think; (b) rephrase the question; (c) ask a related factual question; (d) ask a related interpretive question; (e) ask a related question of evaluation. Finally, as a last resort, call on another student.

5. Leader: Why does Frost have the choice of the less traveled road take place on a fall morning?

Melissa: Fall? It wasn't during fall at all. He made his choice during summer.

Follow-up
question: _____

Comment: *A wrong answer,* that is, an interpretation that cannot be supported by the evidence in the text or which is contradicted by evidence in the text. The coleader has several options: (a) Ask for the supporting that the choice was made during summer. (b) Ask someone else if he or she agrees. (c) Ask a follow-up question for consistency to introduce the contradictory evidence. For example, "Melissa, if he made his choice during summer, why does the first stanza mention a "yellow wood"?" Note: the coleaders must not tell the student that he or she is wrong. Participants must learn to judge for themselves which answers are right or wrong. In short, in Socratic discussion it is essential that students have the freedom to be right and wrong.

6. Leader: In line 16, is the sigh one of satisfaction or regret?

Richard: Satisfaction, of course. That's what the poem is all about.

Follow-up
question: _____

Comment: *The reply is undeveloped and unclear.* Three options: (a) Ask for clarification: "Richard, what is the poem 'all about'?" (b) Get another opinion. (c) Ask a follow-up question for implication: "Richard, do you mean the poem is all about having made a good or bad choice?"

7. Leader: Why will the poet be telling about his decision in the far distant future?

   Mary: Far-distant future? What are you talking about?

   Follow-up
   question: _____

   Comment: The participant does not understand the question. What does a coleader do? The first option (a) ask someone else what the question means; (b) rephrase the question.

8. Leader: Has the choice of the less-traveled road been for better or worse?

   Buster: For sure it has been for the better. That is exactly why he says that he took the less-traveled road, not the one most people would have taken.

   Roger: It has to be for the worse because I think she is trying to talk herself into believing that she did not make a bad choice.

   Rita: Neither. I think the traveler is just saying that he or she made a choice and that was that. It is not a matter of whether a good or bad choice had been made.

   Follow-up
   question: _____

   Comment: *Multiple, rapid responses.* What do the coleaders do? Three options present themselves: (a) Follow-up on any one of the answers but do not ignore them all and merely call on yet another participant. Which one do you pursue? Whatever seems the most interesting and relevant to you. (b) Table on your seating chart one or two responses that you do not immediately pursue and come back to it later. (c) Ask Roger or Buster why he disagrees with Rita's interpretation.

   Note: See summary sheet on the nature and use of spontaneous follow-up questions.

SPONTANEOUS FOLLOW-UP QUESTIONS: GUIDELINES

1. The chief role of the coleaders in discussion is to direct traffic, that is, to direct and control the flow of ideas among the participants. Coleaders fulfill this role by introducing prepared questions to initiate discussion, basic or otherwise, and by asking spontaneous follow-up questions to develop and to connect ideas that help solve the problem(s) under discussion. By following these guidelines, you will lead an effective discussion that increases your own and the group's understanding of the reading. As a result, you will also increase your mutual enjoyment of the reading, the ultimate goal of the Socratic seminar.

2. If you remember that there is no such thing as a perfect or ideal follow-up question, you will not make your role more difficult by trying to second-guess yourself. In other words, there several distinct kinds of follow-up questions that could be asked at any given moment of discussion. The kind of follow-up question asked in specific situation depends on the leader's purpose.

    *   Is it *to clarify*? "What did you mean when you said _____?" or "Could you explain more of what you mean by _____?"

    *   Is it *to substantiate*? "What in the reading are you basing your answer on?" or "How do you know? What in the reading gave your that idea?

    *   Is it *to get more opinion*? For example, "Maria, do you agree with John's view that _____? If so, could you explain? If not, why do you disagree?"

    *   Is it *to test for consistency*? For example, "Sarah, if what you say is correct, then how do you explain _____?"

    *   Is it *to relate* a response to the prepared question? For example, "Brian, how does what you have just said help answer our question about _____?"

    *   Is it *to draw out the implications* of a response? For example, "Ryan, are you saying _____?" "By _____do you mean _____?"

    *   Or finally, is it *to resolve* the prepared question. For example, "John, at this time what is your best answer to our question about _____? Or, "Laura, how many different answers have you heard so far to our basic question?"

3. How often must a leader make a choice about what to pursue, to table, or to ignore? Experience shows that the coleaders must ask an average of one follow-up question for every two or three responses. Unless the coleaders maintain this average by asking enough follow-up questions, or go to the opposite extremes of asking too few or too many follow-up questions, discussion soon reverts to a series of random, unrelated, off-the-cuff comments characteristic of chit-chat.

4

SOCRATIC SEMINARS ON NOVELS AND SHORT STORIES

PREPARING STUDENTS TO PARTICIPATE IN SOCRATIC SEMINARS

The Socratic Seminar is a series of extended discussions focused on a single topic, theme, or series of readings that may or may not be related. The seminar is conducted by a teacher, a team of teachers, or lead by students who have been trained in the Socratic Method (Chapter 3). Its usual length is a full class period of 50 or 90 minutes, two or three days a week. The four rules of Socratic discussion ought to be reviewed first to be sure that the coleaders understand the purpose of each rule—particularly the rule about only asking questions. By following four basic rules, leaders and participants implement a foundation for active learning.

1. *No one may participate who has not read the selection before discussion.* The ticket of admission, is that everyone has read the selection carefully. For this reason, before discussion the leader(s) begin with a plot-check quiz, that is, a list of factual questions that anyone can readily answer if he or she has done the reading. Anyone who has not done the reading is limited to the role of spectator. Note: for less able readers, this rule can be obviated by conducting an oral reading in class (see Stauffer's Directed Reading-Thinking Activity, p. 56).

2. *Participants must support their answers with textual evidence.* Without evidence, discussion soon becomes a matter of sheer conjecture wherein one idea begins to sounds as good as another. Without evidence participants have no way of deciding which answers are better than others and which are wrong. Evidence turns opinion into interpretation. This rule also ensures that everyone has equal

access to the same information on which everyone has to base his or her answers.

3. *Participants may not introduce outside authorities. They can discuss only the assigned reading.* In their *Theory of Literature*, Warren and Welleck get to the heart of the matter:

> The natural sensible starting point for work in literary scholarship is interpretations and analysis of the works of literature themselves. After all, only the works themselves justify all our interest in the life of an author, in his social environment, and the whole process of literature. But curiously enough, literary history has been so preoccupied with the setting of a work of literature that its attempts at analysis of the works themselves have been slight in comparison with the enormous efforts expended on the study of their background.

Furthermore, students learn to become responsible for their own ideas when they do not try to justify them by appealing to an authority—another book or another person. They must learn to rely on their judgment about the meaning of the text itself.

4. *Most important, the leader(s) may only ask questions.* The moment the leader(s) begin making statements during discussion the atmosphere changes from independent thinking and mutual inquiry to attempts to please the leader. Even worse, the vociferous can quickly turn discussion into an argument or debate. Furthermore, no matter how well intentioned, leader comments hinder participants' opportunity to think independently and freely. Finally, the leader's primary role to develop and relate ideas becomes practically impossible when he or she also becomes a participant.

Before students begin to colead discussions, a period should be devoted to the lesson plan that follows to help you to prepare your students for discussion.

PREPARING STUDENTS
FOR A SOCRATIC SEMINAR
LESSON PLAN 4

1. Focus: What questions do you have at this moment about coleading a discussion next week?

2. Objective (what):   To answer all of your questions about coleading. To dispel your doubts about coleading. To develop your confidence as a coleader.

3. Purpose (why):   To prepare you to be effective coleaders so that we increase our mutual understanding and enjoyment of the assigned reading.

4. Input: Review the following handouts: The Four Rules of Socratic Discussion Prediscussion with Your Coleader Guidelines for Coleading Use of the Seating Chart Criteria for Critique of Discussion

5. Modeling: Conduct a 20-minute demonstration discussion with a student coleader on a short reading (e.g., a poem).

6. Checking: Review the demonstration discussion by having students raise questions about how the guidelines were or were not applied.

7. Guided Practice: Review the demonstration discussion by students raise questions about how the guidelines were or were not applied.

8. Closure: Have all your questions about coleading been answered?

Note: This lesson plan is set up for a 50-minute period. If you have a 90-minute period in a block schedule, you could extend modeling by conducting a 20-minute demonstration discussion during which you explain why you are asking some of the follow-up questions as you go along.

THE SOCRATIC SEMINAR:
COLEADING DISCUSSION GUIDELINES

When you colead a 15-minute discussion of an assigned reading, please follow these guidelines to insure that discussion is truly a mutual learning experience.

- ♦ Sit next to your coleader and make out a *seating chart* from your position in the group.

- ♦ Have the group *write down* your prepared question, basic or otherwise, on a piece of paper and give them about three minutes to jot down a brief, initial response.

- ♦ The leaders and the group must observe the *four rules of discussion:*
    1. No one may participate who has not read the text.
    2.   Discuss only the text that everyone has read.
    3. *The coleaders may only ask questions and must avoid statements of any kind.*
    4. Do not bring in outside authorities to support your answers. Rely on the text for evidence.

- ♦ Begin the discussion by calling on someone *by name* to give his or her answer. Address all questions to people by name to control the flow of discussion. Although participants may speak up freely without being called on, the coleaders must recognize them by name to direct the group's attention.

- ♦ Make every effort to *call on everyone* in your group at least once or twice. Put a mark next to the name on your seating chart every time that you call on someone to respond. *Try to avoid calling on the same few participants too often or not calling on some individuals at all.*

- ♦ For every two or three responses, you and your coleader should be asking a spontaneous follow-up question to develop the ideas given and to keep the group's thinking focused on your prepared question.

- ♦ At the end of 15 minutes, ask individuals in the group to recall briefly the different answers that have been given to your prepared question. Note these answers in brief on your seating chart and hand in at the end of class.

- ♦ The answers to your prepared question noted on your seating chart are the degree to which you have *increased your own and the group's understanding of the reading*—the goal of shared inquiry. This is the *resolution* of discussion; it is an individual matter, not a group consensus.

PREPARING QUESTIONS WITH YOUR COLEADER: GUIDELINES FOR PRE-DISCUSSION

♦ Before meeting with your coleader, each of you should have 15 or 20 interpretive questions with a page reference for each whenever possible. The page references make it easier for you both to turn to the page that gave you the idea for the question. Page references also help you to make your questions specific.

♦ Begin the pre-discussion by checking the wording of your questions. Do this by applying the Qualities of Good Discussion Questions: Checklist for Evaluating Questions (p. 33). If you cannot revise your questions to have these six characteristics, drop them. If you have trouble getting to your deepest level of understanding (that is, writing questions that have real doubt for you) review the handout on the Three Levels of Doubt (p. 36).

♦ At this point you should decide if you want to go with a list of at least 10 good interpretive questions (arranged in any order that seems logical to you) or decide to write a basic question similar to those that accompany the lesson plan for each reading. Indeed, you may want to try out one of the suggested basic questions that lack follow-up questions and see if together you can come up with a cluster of at least 8 interpretive follow-up questions.

♦ Agree on the question you want to use to open your discussion. Do not be overly concerned with your choice of an opening question. Any question you both genuinely care about is suitable.

Two Important Caveats

♦ If you do not have a pre-discussion with your coleader before each discussion meeting, you cannot expect to have a good experience. In failing to carry out your responsibility to the group, you fail yourself. If you enjoy coleading and want to increase your skill to become a good discussion leader who inspires students to read and learn from one another, pre-discussion is imperative.

♦ The model basic questions that accompany the lesson plan for each reading are *not* intended to be ready-made questions for you to try out on a group. The issues they raise and the inquiries they pose are meant to make you think harder and better about *your* questions. To be sure, next to asking good spontaneous follow-up questions, the hardest part of the Socratic method is coming up with your own questions about the readings. Why? There are no answer keys for discussion and because thinking *is* difficult! Nevertheless, the rewards are great.

THE SEATING CHART:
ITS USE AND IMPORTANCE

At the beginning of each discussion, it is important that the coleaders make a seating chart from their position in the group. The participants should be seated in a circle. The seating chart has three important functions:

1. It locates each participant and enables you to call on each person by name. Preface all your questions by using an individual's name.

    -   This helps you control the discussion.

    -   If all have responsibility for a question, usually no one does.

    -   It gives the person who is called on a few seconds to think of an answer. In theory, everyone should be prepared to speak all the time, but in practice, it seldom works out that way.

    -   It enables you to call on those less likely to speak up on their own. Throwing a question out to everyone usually results in verbally aggressive participants taking over.

2. It enables the coleaders to involve all participants more or less equally.

    -   During a 15- to 30-minute segment of discussion, the coleaders should try to call on everyone at least once, ideally twice.

    -   The coleaders should ask an average of one follow-up question for every two or three responses.

3. It enables the coleaders to exercise their options: to ignore, to table, and to pursue responses.

    -   Next to the names of participants, the coleaders can jot down those ideas they are pursuing immediately and to table those questions for later discussion.

    -   Because it is impossible to follow-up on every idea in discussion, the coleaders must make conscious choices about what they pursue immediately, table for later, or ignore. Unless they do so, they begin to pick up on the last remark of the last participant. When this happens, discussion degenerates into a series of unrelated comments.

CRITERIA FOR CRITIQUE OF DISCUSSION
IN THE SOCRATIC SEMINAR

Coleaders: _____ and _____ English _____
Reading _____ Date _____
Question _____

Code: Good (10)   Pretty good (5)   Needs improvement (0)

1. Did the leaders initiate discussion by beginning   10   5   0
    with a *good interpretive question?*

2. Did the leaders call on *all* participants at least   10   5   0
    once?

3. Did the leaders *average* one follow-up question for 10   5   0
    every two or three responses?

4. Did the leaders *avoid making statements* or asking   10   5   0
    leading questions?

5. Did the leaders seek *clarification* as well as *substan-* 10   5   0
    tiation when necessary?

6. Did the leaders *colead*? Did they share equally the   10   5   0
    task of asking follow-up questions?

7. Did the leaders get answers to *questions on the*   10   5   0
    floor before moving on to new ideas?

8. Did the leaders *stick to* their prepared questions?   10   5   0

9. Did the leaders *pick up* ideas from the participants 10   5   0
    for follow-up questions? Or, if they began with a
    basic question, did they rely too much on their list
    of prepared follow-up questions?

10. Did the leaders *resolve* their prepared question?   10   5   0

    TOTALS   (___/100)

STAUFFER'S DIRECTED
READING-THINKING ACTIVITY

Developed and made popular by Russell Stauffer, the directed reading-teaching activity (DR-TA) remains one of the most effective and useful in-class exercises for a first reading of a short story or poem. This directed reading and thinking exercise is a five-step process:

1. Identifies a purpose for the reading.

2. Adjusts the reading rate to its purpose and material.

3. Observes the reading sequentially.

4. Develops initial comprehension.

5. Trains in basic reading and thinking skills.

In the first step, having read the title and any subheading, the teacher asks students to predict what they expect to find in the reading. By doing this, students become aware of their prior knowledge and think about what they may already know about the subject of the reading. In short, each student sets a purpose for the reading by anticipating what he or she will find in the text. A student then checks, by reading and rereading the text, if his or her predictions turn out to be true.

In the second step, students continue to confirm and refine their predictions as more of the text is revealed. Their rate of reading depend on their individual purposes as they seek to confirm and revise their expectations.

In step three, the teacher observes students' involvement with the reading and their ability to adjust their rates of reading according to their purposes. The teacher offers to help those having difficulty with unfamiliar vocabulary or ideas by asking appropriate and relevant follow-up questions.

The teacher's role in the fourth step is to help students adjust their rates of reading by judicious use of follow-up questions designed to help them clarify, substantiate, and develop their responses by drawing out their implications. In short, the teacher's role in this step is to expand student responses.

The final and fifth step is concerned with fundamental skill-training activities that include the most important second, and silent, reading. The second reading is then followed by a 30-minute discussion of the entire reading that is in turn is followed by a writing activity.

NOTE: For an extended explanation of Stauffer's process, see Jane L. Davidson, "The DR-TA: A Reading-Thinking Strategy for All Levels," *Reading as Language Experience*, Connecticut: University of Connecticut, 1979, 37–43. See also Bonnie Greenslade, "Awareness and Anticipation: Utilizing the DR-TR in the Content Classroom," *Journal of Language Experience*, Vol. 2, No. 2, 1980, 21–28.

THE ZEBRA STORYTELLER
LESSON PLAN 5:
DIRECTED READING-THINKING ACTIVITY

1.	Focus:	What was the best joke (or funny short short story) that you have ever heard? After you first heard it, did you want to tell someone else about it? If so, why?
2.	Objective:	To define and illustrate the five-step process of the DR–TA.
3.	Purpose:	To model a first-reading of a story with an entire class.
		To prepare students for a second reading and discussion of the entire story.
4.	Input:	*The Zebra Storyteller* (put on overhead projector [OH]).
5.	Modeling:	Conduct a demonstration discussion of the first reading of *The Zebra Storyteller.*
		See the model follow-up questions for each segment of the story.
6.	Checking for understanding:	Give students time to think about how to answer some of your prepared and spontaneous follow-up questions on the story.
7.	Guided practice:	Ask prepared and spontaneous follow-up questions as needed during the reading.
8.	Closure:	What is the value of this first reading?
		Why do we need a second reading before further discussion?

Note: Because *The Zebra Storyteller* raises a basic question about the value of storytelling, a timely follow-up lesson might include a discussion of the value of reading and studying imaginative literature. See Lesson Plan 6: *What is the Value of Reading Literature.*

THE ZEBRA STORYTELLER

Spencer Holst

*(Handout for after the first group reading for a second,
silent reading and notations)*

Once upon a time there was a Siamese cat who pretended to be a lion and spoke inappropriate Zebraic.

That language is whinnied by the race of striped horses in Africa.

Here now: An innocent zebra is walking in a jungle and approaching from another direction is the little cat; they meet.

"Hello there!" says the Siamese cat in perfectly pronounced Zebraic. "It certainly is a pleasant day, isn't it? The sun is shining, the birds are singing; isn't the world a lovely place to live today?"

The zebra is so astonished at hearing a Siamese cat speaking like a zebra, why—he's fit to be tied.

So the little cat quickly ties him up, kills him, and drags the better parts of the carcass back to his den.

The cat successfully hunted zebras many months in this manner, dining on filet mignon of zebra every night, and from the better hides he made bow ties and wide belts after the fashion of the decadent princes of the Old Siamese court.

He began boasting to his friends he was a lion, and he gave them as proof the fact that he hunted zebras.

The delicate noses of the zebras told them there was really no lion in the neighborhood. The zebra deaths caused many to avoid the region. Superstitious, they decided the woods were haunted by the ghost of a lion.

One day the storyteller of the zebras was ambling, and through his mind ran plots for stories to amuse the other zebras, when suddenly he eyes brightened, and he said, "That's it! I'll tell a story about a Siamese cat who learns to speak our language! What an idea! That'll make 'em laugh!"

Just then the Siamese cat appeared before him, and said, "Hello there! Pleasant day today, isn't it?"

The zebra storyteller wasn't fit to be tied at hearing a cat speaking his language, because he'd been thinking about that very thing.

He took a good look at the cat, and he didn't know what, but there was some-thing about his looks he didn't like, so he kicked him with a hoof and killed him.

That is the function of a storyteller.

Source: Spencer, W. (1993). *The Zebra Storyteller: Collected Stories.* Barrytown, NY: Station Hill Press.

SAMPLE PREPARED FOLLOW-UP QUESTIONS FOR A DR–TA: *THE ZEBRA STORYTELLER*

Title

---

1. What is the story going to be about?
2. What kind of story could you tell about telling stories?
3. What is a Zebra storyteller?

Once upon a time there was a Siamese cat who pretended to be a lion and spoke inappropriate Zebraic.

That language is whinnied by the race of striped horses in Africa.

---

4. Who is the story teller?
5. Why would a Siamese cat tell stories to zebras?
6. What is distinctive or unusual about Siamese cats?
7. What is "inappropriate" about a cat speaking Zebraic?

Here now: An innocent zebra is walking in a jungle and approaching from another direction is the little cat; they meet.

"Hello there!" says the Siamese cat in perfectly pronounced Zebraic. "It certainly is a pleasant day, isn't it? The sun is shining, the birds are singing; isn't the world a lovely place to live today?"

---

8. Why does the cat speak Zebraic perfectly and yet we are told that this is "inappropriate"?
9. Will the Zebra answer the cat's questions?
10. How will the Zebra react to the cat's friendly greeting?

The zebra is so astonished at hearing a Siamese cat speaking like a zebra, why—he's fit to be tied.

---

11. Why is the zebra so astonished at the cat's greeting him in zebra?
12. What does "he's fit to be tied" mean?
13. How will the cat respond to the Zebra's amazement?

So the little cat quickly ties him up, kills him, and drags the better parts of the carcass back to his den.

The cat successfully hunted zebras many months in this manner, dining on filet mignon of zebra every night, and from the better hides he made bow ties and wide belts after the fashion of the decadent princes of the Old Siamese court.

14. Was your prediction correct? Why? Why not?

15. Why is the cat able to tie up a zebra?

16. Why does the cat kill the zebra?

17. Why is the cat fashion conscious?

18. What will the cat do next?

He began boasting to his friends he was a lion, and he gave them as proof the fact that he hunted zebras.

19. Was your prediction correct about the cat's reaction? Why? Why not?

20. How will the zebra's react to the cat's boast that he was a lion?

The delicate noses of the zebras told them there was really no lion in the neighborhood. The zebra deaths caused many to avoid the region. Superstitious, they decided the woods were haunted by the ghost of a lion.

21. Was your prediction correct about the zebra's reaction to the cat's boast and "proof" that he was a lion?

22. Will the zebras do anything more than avoid the woods?

One day the storyteller of the zebras was ambling, and through his mind ran plots for stories to amuse the other zebras, when suddenly he eyes brightened, and he said, "That's it! I'll tell a story about a Siamese cat who learns to speak our language! What an idea! That'll make 'em laugh!"

23. Why does the Zebra storyteller tell stories?

24. What will happen next? How do you know?

Just then the Siamese cat appeared before him, and said, "Hello there! Pleasant day today, isn't it?"

25. Was your prediction correct?

26. How will the Zebra storyteller react to the cat's friendly greeting?

The zebra storyteller wasn't fit to be tied at hearing a cat speaking his language, because he'd been thinking about that very thing.

He took a good look at the cat, and he didn't know what, but there was something about his looks he didn't like, so he kicked him with a hoof and killed him.

---

27. Was your prediction correct? Why? Why not?

28. Why does the zebra kill the cat?

29. Were you surprised that the zebra killed the cat? Why? Why not?

30. What is the last sentence of the story?

That is the function of a storyteller.

---

31. Was your prediction correct? Why? Why not?

32. What is the job of a storyteller?

Source: Spencer, W. (1993). *The Zebra Storyteller: Collected Stories*. Barrytown, NY: Station Hill Press.

WHAT IS THE VALUE OF READING AND STUDYING LITERATURE?

Because *The Zebra Storyteller* raises a basic question about the value of storytelling, a timely follow-up lesson is a discussion of the good or value of reading and even studying imaginative literature.

WHAT IS THE VALUE OF READING LITERATURE?
LESSON PLAN 6

1. Focus: Journal topic: For you, what is the value of reading and studying stories?

2. Objective: To compare and contrast several answers to the basic question after writing about it in the journal.

3. Purpose: To discover why this question is fundamental to an English class.

4. Input: List differing student answers to the journal question on the overhead. Then have them read the article by Moeller (handout; see p. 63). Ask them to choose the single most important reason for reading and study that they found in the article.

5. Modeling: Review Moeller's answers to the basic question by asking students: Which of the six reasons meant the most to you? Why?

6. Checking and guided practice: Ask for an example of some story that illustrates each of the reasons in the article.

7. Closure: Review what they now regard as the most important reason for reading and studying literature. Write a one-page essay to hand in at the next class meeting.

WHY DO WE READ AND EVEN STUDY LITERATURE?

Victor J. Moeller

1. The most obvious reason has to be that stories are *entertaining and amusing.* With imaginative literature, there is something to satisfy everyone's taste— from romance, to gothic tales, to mystery, to westerns, to science-fiction, to whatever! Look around. Be a browser. Talk to a reader.

2. Reading stories also *educates our imaginations.* Those who think that a story like *The Zebra Storyteller* is dumb or stupid, have not developed their imaginations. In fiction, anything can happen and an author does not have to prove anything. Our only obligation as readers is to understand the world that an author has placed us in—not to argue about the author's creation. If we make a sincere effort to understand, we can increase our enjoyment immensely. Unless we develop our imaginations, we will remain literal-minded and foolishly demand that all stories be true-to-life. How dull that would be.

3. On the other hand, the contrast between the real or actual and the extraordinary or fanciful, suggests two different uses that readers make of imaginative literature. Sometimes we *do* want to read about people like ourselves, or about places, things, experiences, and ideas that we are familiar with and that make us feel comfortable. In the process of reading about situations related to our own lives, *we can learn more about ourselves and the world around us.* Realism always has an appeal.

4. But at other times, the last thing that we want is a story about people like ourselves or experiences similar to those in our own everyday lives. We might even be accused of wanting *to escape.* We want something *different or strange*— like Stephen King stories. We want to get out of ourselves and the all-too-familiar, and learn that there are other ways of looking at the world besides our own. In short, we want to read about exotic places, about other worlds that have never existed, or worlds that may never exist. In other words, the romantic spirit always contends with the appeal of realism.

5. Stories also *prepare us for the unexpected and help us avoid projecting false hopes and fears* (such as superstitious zebras who think that they are being preyed on by ghosts of lions) and show us what we can expect in our everyday lives. Because some people never train their imagination to project any "story" other than their own, they cannot conceive of any other shape for their expectations. As a result, they remain stunted and naive about life.

6. Finally, *reading stories can put us in closer touch with our feelings.* Good stories, powerful stories, *revulse us* with what is ugly and cruel and mean in life. On the other hand, stories can also *inspire us* to marvel at what is good and wonderful and beautiful in life. For example, recall George's devotion to Lennie (*Of Mice and Men*) or Nick Carraway's refusal to become as self-serving as those about him (*The Great Gatsby*). In short, some stories can be so terrible that they may move us to tears and prompt us to say, "That's the way life must never be," while others are so poignant that we find ourselves saying, "That's the way life ought to be," or, "That's the way life could be!"

SOCRATIC SEMINAR
LESSON PLAN 7:
THE PIGMAN:

1. Focus:

Journal writing: Who is the most unusual grown-up that you have ever had a long-term relationship with? How would you describe him or her to someone else who has never met this person?

2. Objective:

To resolve three or four basic questions of interpretation about the overall meanings of the novel.

3. Purpose:

To develop the habit of independent and reflective thinking. To increase our mutual understanding and enjoyment of the novel.

4. Input:

Begin with a factual quiz (pp. 65–70) on each of the three parts of the novel. Three or four basic questions (pp. 71–73)

5. Modeling, checking, and guided practice:

During discussion the student coleaders and/or the teacher model the four rules of Socratic discussion. Check for understanding by asking follow-up questions for clarification, substantiation, consistency, relevance, implication, resolution, and to get more opinions. Guided practice *is* the discussion.

6. Closure:

Written resolution (one-page essay) of one of the basic questions just discussed.

Note: During Socratic Seminar day(s), in a full 90-minute period, four pairs of student coleaders each lead a 15-minute discussion of the reading. The teacher must approve in advance student coleader questions to avoid wasting time on questions that are not clear, factual, or evaluative. (Discussion should center on solving problems, not in trying to figure out what the problems are.)

Reading: Zindel, Paul. *The Pigman.* Bantam. New York, 1969 (149 pages).

THE PIGMAN: QUIZ
PLOT-CHECK CHAPTERS 1–5

English _____ Name _____ SCORE: _____/50

Directions: Answer each question in the space beneath it in *complete* sentences. Do not cross out answers.

1. What kind of "kid stuff" did John do in school as a freshman? Be specific.

2. How does John get around using profanity in telling his story?

3. According to Lorraine, what is a big difference between herself and John?

4. What did John and Lorraine do on the school bus that made them seem strange?

5. What was the object of John and Lorraine's telephone game?

6. How did Lorraine and John first make contact with the Pigman?

7. Why is Norton called the Marshmallow Kid?

8. What did Miss Truman and John Fund first ask Mr. Pignati to do for them?

9. What doesn't John like about Kenneth?

10. When John and Lorraine first meet Mr. Pignati in person, what do they immediately like about him?

Score: 5x10=50 points possible

Grader's name _____ (print in pencil)

THE PIGMAN: QUIZ
PLOT-CHECK CHAPTERS 1–5: ANSWER KEY

Directions: Answer each question in the space beneath it in *complete* sentences. Do not cross-out answers.

1. What kind of "kid stuff" did John do in school as a freshman? Be specific. (pp. 1–3)

    As the Bathroom Bomber, he set off firecrackers. He also organized "fruit rolls," usually when substitute teachers took over the class.

2. How does John get around using profanity in telling his story? (p. 5)

    He used numbers and symbols. For example, 3@#$% meant a really bad curse.

3. According to Lorraine, what is a big difference between herself and John? (pp. 8–9)

    She is compassionate while John pretends he doesn't care about anything.

4. What did John and Lorraine do on the school bus that made them seem strange? (p. 13)

    They began laughing together uncontrollably and loudly.

5. What was the object of John and Lorraine's telephone game? (p. 15)

    After choosing a number at random, they tried to see how long they could keep a stranger talking on the phone. (The record was almost two and a half hours.)

6. How did Lorraine and John first make contact with the Pigman? (p.18)

    To play a prank, they took his name at random out of the phone book.

7. Why is Norton called the Marshmallow Kid? (p. 19)

    His name was published in the paper for shop lifting a bag of marshmallows.

8. What did Miss Truman and John Fund first ask Mr. Pignati to do for them? (p. 24)

    They asked him to send them money for the L and J Fund.

9. What doesn't John like about Kenneth? (p. 27)

    He doesn't like his older brother because his parents favor him and hold him up as a model of a successful money maker on Wall Street.

10. When John and Lorraine first meet Mr. Pignati in person, what did they immediately like about him? (p. 32)

    His big smile made him look as though he was genuinely glad to see them at his door.

Score: 5x10=50 points possible

Grader's name _____ (print in pencil)

THE PIGMAN: QUIZ
PLOT-CHECK CHAPTERS 6–10

English _____ Name _____ SCORE: _____/50

Directions: Answer each question in the space beneath it in *complete* sentences. Do not cross-out answers.

1.   What does Lorraine's mother steal from some of her patients?

2.   What is distinctive about the description of Bobo?

3.   What is John concerned about when he is talking to the stars in the cemetery?

4.   What does John's mother tell him to do after tells his father he wants to be an actor when he grows up?

5.   What does Lorraine think about her father and mother's relationship after thinking about Mr. Pignati's and Conchetta's marriage?

6.   How does Lorraine describe the experience of buying roller skates with an old man?

7.   What will always make Norton very angry?

8.   How does John explain why he started drinking?

9.   What does Lorraine's mother fail to do after Lorraine gives her new stockings?

10. How does Mr. Pignati change as he spends more and more time with the kids?

Score: 5x10=50 points possible

Grader's name _____ (print in pencil)

THE PIGMAN: QUIZ
PLOT-CHECK QUIZ CHAPTERS 6–10: ANSWER KEY

Directions: Answer each question in the space beneath it in *complete* sentences. Do not cross-out answers.

1.   What does Lorraine's mother steal from some of her patients?

     She steals food and canned goods from her patients.

2.   What is distinctive about the description that is given of Bobo?

     Bobo is the ugliest, meanest, and most vicious-looking baboon in the monkey house.

3.   What is John concerned about when he is talking to the stars in the cemetery?

     John worries that there may be no spiritual life after a physical death.

4.   What does John's mother tell him to do after he tells his father he wants to be an actor when he grows up?

     She tells him that he should go to a friend's house because his father may be upset.

5.   What does Lorraine think about her father and mother's relationship after thinking about Mr. Pignati's and Conchetta's marriage?

     She thinks that her own father may never really have loved her mother.

6.   How does Lorraine describe the experience of buying roller skates with an old man?

     She describes it as *silly, absurd, and beautiful.*

7.   What will always make Norton very angry?

     He gets very angry whenever anyone calls him The Marshmallow Kid.

8.   How does John explain why he started drinking?

     He explains it was one of the few things that his father ever said that he did well and it got him attention from all the other guests.

9.   What doesn't Lorraine's mother do after Lorraine gives her the new stockings?

     She doesn't thank her daughter for the gift.

10. How does Mr. Pignati change as he spends more and more time with the kids?

     Mr. Pignati becomes more and more kid-like.

Score: 5x10=50 points possible

Grader's name _____ (print in pencil)

THE PIGMAN: QUIZ
PLOT-CHECK CHAPTERS 11–15

English _____ Name _____ SCORE: _____/50

Directions: Answer each question in the space beneath it in *complete* sentences. Do not cross-out answers.

1. What is Mr. Pignati's biggest concern when John and Lorraine visit him in the hospital?

2. What do John and Lorraine do immediately after their first kiss in Mr. Pignati's bedroom?

3. What does Lorraine think about when she is eating dinner with John in Mr. Pignati's home?

4. What does John decide to do after having a fight with Lorraine about cleaning up?

5. Why did Janice Dickery have to drop out of school early?

6. In what condition is the oscilloscope that Norton tries to steal as soon as he gets to the party?

7. What does Mr. Pignati do when he sees his house has been wrecked?

8. What happens to Mr. Pignati shortly after he learns of Bobo's death?

9. What does Lorraine say that John and Lorraine have done to Mr. Pignati?

10. What does John think Mr. Pignati had done that older people are not supposed to do?

Score: 5x10=50 points possible

Grader's name _____ (print in pencil)

THE PIGMAN: QUIZ
PLOT-CHECK CHAPTERS 11–15—ANSWER KEY

Directions: Answer each question in the space beneath it in *complete* sentences. Do not cross-out answers.

1. What is Mr. Pignatti's biggest concern when John and Lorraine visit him in the hospital?

    He is most concerned about who will take care of feeding Bobo.

2. What do John and Lorraine do immediately after their first kiss in Mr. Pignati's bedroom?

    Lorraine said it was time to go downstairs for dinner and John agreed.

3. What does Lorraine think about when she is eating dinner with John in Mr. Pignati's home?

    She thinks about a future married life with someone you love.

4. What does John decide to do after having a fight with Lorraine about cleaning up?

    He decides to have some friends over for a drinking party.

5. Why did Janice Dickery have to drop out of school early?

    She became pregnant.

6. In what condition is the oscilloscope that Norton tries to steal as soon as he gets to the party?

    The old oscilloscope is a piece of useless junk.

7. What does Mr. Pignatti do when he sees his house has been wrecked?

    He starts to cry.

8. What happens to Mr. Pignati shortly after he learns of Bobo's death?

    He also dies.

9. What does Lorraine say that John and Lorraine have done to Mr. Pignatti?

    She thinks that they have murdered him!

10. What does John think Mr. Pignati had done that older people are not supposed to do?

    John thinks that Mr. Pignatti has "trespassed" on the ground of younger people.

Score: 5x10=50 points possible

Grader's name _____ (print in pencil)

BASIC QUESTIONS: *THE PIGMAN*

BASIC QUESTION OF INTERPRETATION 1

Do John and Lorraine like Mr. Pignati so much chiefly because he is so accepting of them?

If *yes*, then:

1. Why is Lorraine's mother portrayed as overly protective?

2. Why does it bother Lorraine so much when her mother asks her if Mr. Pignati had tried to abuse her?

3. Why is John's mother portrayed as more concerned with cleanliness than with her son's drinking and smoking?

4. Why is John's father portrayed as concerned only with making a living?

5. Why does John's father want John to become like his brother, Kenneth?

6. Unlike Lorraine, why does John have refer to his parents as "The Old Lady" and "the Bore"?

7. Why does John's father ridicule John's dream to become an actor?

8. Why do both Lorraine and John think their parents do not understand them?

9. Why can't Lorraine tell her mother that she wants to become a writer?

10. Why does John tell us in the first sentence of the story that his dislike for school was a factor in getting involved with the Pigman?

11. Does Zindel want us to agree with Lorraine's assessment of her mother as a bitter woman who has been betrayed by her husband?

12. Does Zindel want us to agree with John's assessment of his parents as two people who never really loved each other?

If *no*, then:

13. Why do John and Lorraine begin visiting Mr. Pignati almost daily?

14. Why are both John and Lorraine impressed at Mr. Pignati's friendliness?

15. Why are John and Lorraine more at home with Mr. Pignati than with their parents?

16. Why do John and Lorraine change from taking advantage of Mr. Pignati to showing genuine concern for him?

17. Why do John and Lorraine have so much fun playing with Mr. Pignati?

BASIC QUESTION OF INTERPRETATION 2

Why does Zindel have John and Lorraine alternate as narrator for each chapter?

1. Why does the story begin with "The Oath"?

2. What do John and Lorraine mean by recording "the facts, and only the facts" about their encounter with Mr. Pignati?

3. Why do John and Lorraine refer to their story as a "memorial epic"?

4. Why does Zindel begin and end the story with John as narrator?

5. What is the chief difference between the way Lorraine and John tell the story?

6. Does Zindel portray Lorraine as more sensible than John?

7. Does Zindel portray John as more compassionate than Lorraine?

8. Why does Lorraine say that she should not have allowed John to write the first chapter?

BASIC QUESTION OF INTERPRETATION 3

Does Zindel want us to agree with John's assessment of Mr. Pignati's life as a lonely old man reduced to begging for friends? (p. 144)

If *yes*, then:

1. Does Mr. Pignati ever accept his wife's death?

2. Why does Mr. Pignati keep his wife's clothes in her closet?

3. Why does Mr. Pignati at first deny his wife's death but then admit it?

4. Why does Mr. Pignati have such an elaborate collection of pigs?

5. What does Zindel mean when he says that he had Mr. Pignati die because "the story just seemed to point that way"? (p. 156)

6. Does Mr. Pignati accept John and Lorraine because he needs them or because he suspects that they may need him? (is this a better phrasing of the BQ?)

7. Why doesn't Mr. Pignati say anything when John and Lorraine confess that they had been playing a game by being charity workers?

8. Why doesn't Mr. Pignati have press charges against John and Lorraine for trashing his house?

9. Why does Lorraine blame John for Mr. Pignati's first heart attack?

If *no*, then:

10. Why does Mr. Pignati do so much to please John and Lorraine?

11. Why does Mr. Pignati serve wine to underage teenagers?

12. Why does Mr. Pignati show his prize pig collection to John and Lorraine?

13. Why is feeding and visiting Bobo so important to Mr. Pignati?

14. Why does Mr. Pignati die when Bobo dies?

BASIC QUESTION OF INTERPRETATION 4

Why are John Coleman and Lorraine Jensen so attracted to each other?

1. What makes Lorraine fall in love with John?

2. When does John begin to try to impress Lorraine?

3. Why does the story begin with Lorraine talking about John's lack of compassion but end with John remaining with Mr. Pignati when Mr. Pignati dies?

4. Why does Zindel want us to know that Lorraine has no pretensions about her beauty?

5. When does Lorraine first recognize the good in John?

6. Does John like Lorraine because she is as zany as he is?

7. Are John and Lorraine more alike than different?

8. Why do both John and Lorraine have parents who do not really understand them?

GOOD COUNTRY PEOPLE
LESSON PLAN 8

1. Focus:
Begin with a factual quiz of ten questions to ensure that those who participate in the discussions have read the story. (15 minutes)

2. Objective:
To solve several questions of interpretation about the overall meaning of the short story.

3. Purpose:
To increase our mutual understanding (comprehension) and, as a result, our enjoyment of the story.

4. Input:
Begin with a review quiz on the six qualities of good discussion questions. (15 minutes) See handout. Two or four basic questions. (30 or 60 minutes)

5. Modeling, checking, and guided practice:
During discussion the coleaders model the four rules of discussion, check for understanding by asking follow-up questions for clarification, substantiation, consistency, relevance, implication, resolution, and to get more opinion. Guided practice is the discussion.

6. Closure:
Oral or written resolution of one or two basic questions just discussed.

Note: During Socratic Seminar day(s), in a full 90-minute period, four pairs of student coleaders each lead a 15-minute discussion of the reading. It is important that the teacher approves the student coleader questions before discussion to avoid wasting time on questions that are not clear, factual, or evaluative. (Discussion should center on solving problems, not in trying to figure out what the problems are.) During the remaining time (if any) the teacher leads a demonstration discussion (modeling) of one of his or her basic questions on the reading of the lesson.

Reading: O'Connor, Flannery (1970). *A Good Man Is Hard to Find and Other Stories.* Garden City, New York, Doubleday & Co.

BASIC QUESTIONS: *GOOD COUNTRY PEOPLE*

BASIC QUESTION OF INTERPRETATION 1

Does Hula reject Manley Pointer's sexual advances mainly because she would not have been in control of the situation?

If *yes*, then:

1. Why does Hulga at first think that her meeting Manley is a joke but then begin to see "profound implications" in it? (p. 254)

2. Why does Hulga at first lie about her age to Manley but later tell him the truth? (pp. 254, 258)

3. If Hulga believed in "nothing," why does she tell Manley that there must be no dishonesty between them? (p. 258)

4. According to the narrator, what "truth" about Hulga had Manley touched? (p. 259)

5. Why does Hulga get so upset when Manley puts a contraceptive in her hand? (p. 260)

6. Why does Hulga think that SHE had seduced Manley when he asked her to prove her love for him? (p. 259)

7. Why does Hulga pleadingly ask Manley if he was just good country people? (p. 260)

8. Why didn't Hulga want to feel dependent on Manley? (p. 260)

If *no*, then:

9. Why does Hulga have a fantasy about seducing Manley? (p. 255)

10. In her fantasy, why does Hulga regard Manley as having an inferior mind? (p. 255)

11. When Hulga agrees to go on a picnic with Manley, why does she suggest that they go to an old barn? (p. 255)

12. What does Hulga mean when she tells Manley that she loved him "in a sense"? (p. 258)

13. Why does Hulga think SHE had seduced Manley when he asked her to prove her love for him? (p. 259)

14. When Manley himself took off Hulga's leg, why does she have a fantasy about running away with him? (p. 259)

15. Why does Hulga demand that Manley put her leg back on? (p. 260)

16. Why does Joy get so angry when she realizes that Manley was "a perfect Christian" just "like them all"? (p. 261)

BASIC QUESTION OF INTERPRETATION 2

Why does the narrator want us to know that both Hulga and Manley are atheists and that they both have heart conditions? (pp. 249, 251, 256, 261)

1. Why did Hulga's mother agree not to keep a Bible in the parlor because her daughter was an atheist? (p. 249)

2. Does Hulga's mother ask Manley to stay for dinner only because he told her of his heart condition? (p. 251)

3. When Manley tells Hulga of his heart condition, why does she suddenly tell him that she might also die prematurely? (p. 255)

4. When Manley tells Hulga that God must be taking care of her, why does she tell him that she doesn't even believe in God? (p. 256)

5. In reply what does Manley mean when he tells Hulga that it is unusual for a girl not to believe in God? (p. 256)

6. At this point in the story, why doesn't Manley scold Hulga for being at atheist? (p. 256)

7. Why does Manley tell Hulga that HE had believed "in nothing" since birth? (p. 261)

8. Why does Hulga get so angry when she discovers that Manley is "perfect" hypocritical Christian just like them all? (p. 261)

9. Is Hulga an atheist because she thinks many Christians are hypocrites? (p. 261)

10. Does Manley equate believing "in nothing" with not believing in God? (p. 261)

AN ALTERNATIVE BASIC QUESTION

Here is another basic question that you can qualify for discussion if you can come up with at least eight related interpretive follow-up questions for each. When students are struggling to write their own basic questions, I sometimes "give" them a basic question as an intermediate step to writing their own clusters. They then have to develop at least eight of their own related interpretive follow-up questions.

BASIC QUESTION OF INTERPRETATION 3

Why is Joy so angry with her mother?

QUALITIES OF GOOD DISCUSSION QUESTIONS:
GOOD COUNTRY PEOPLE—REVIEW QUIZ

Directions: Apply these criteria *in the order given* to this list of questions. Put the code letters at the left that best apply to each question.

NC: not clear

NS: not specific

NIF: not interpretive but factual

GO: for good or satisfactory

NIE: not interpretive but evaluative

NA: not answerable on the basis of the story alone

LD: lacks doubt

_____ 1.   What is ironic about Mrs. Hopewell's daughter?

_____ 2.   How would you describe Hulga's relationship with her mother?

_____ 3.   What is the role of Mrs. Freeman in this story?

_____ 4.   What symbolic meanings do the characters' names have? (Hopewell, Freeman, Hulga, Joy)

_____ 5.   Do the characters' names have any significance (Hopewell, Freeman, Hulga, and Joy)?

_____ 6.   How did Hulga lose her leg?

_____ 7.   Why does the story begin with a character sketch of Mrs. Freeman?

_____ 8.   Is O'Connor using Hulga (Joy) Hopewell?

_____ 9.   Why is Hulga so angry with her mother?

_____ 10. Why does Mrs. Hopewell think young women go to college?

_____ 11. If Joy is really a philosopher why is she so rude?

_____ 12. Why does Joy look down on young men?

Score: 5x12=_____/60

Grader's name _____ (print in pencil)

QUALITIES OF GOOD DISCUSSION QUESTIONS:
GOOD COUNTRY PEOPLE—REVIEW QUIZ
ANSWER KEY

Directions: Apply these criteria *in the order given* to this list of questions. Put the code letters at the left that best apply to each question.

NC: not clear

NS: not specific

NIF: not interpretive but factual

GO: for good or satisfactory

NIE: not interpretive but evaluative

NA: not answerable on the basis of the story alone

LD: lacks doubt

NC 1. What is ironic about Mrs. Hopewell's daughter?
How does irony apply to Mrs. Hopewell's daughter, Joy?

NS 2. How would you describe Hulga's relationship with her mother?
Could be asked of any two characters in any story.

NS 3. What is the role of Mrs. Freeman in this story?
Can be asked of any character in any story

GO 4. What symbolic meanings do the characters' names have? (Hopewell, Freeman, Hulga, Joy)

LD 5. Do the characters' names have any significance (Hopewell, Freeman, Hulga, and Joy)?
Yes, they have significance. See question 4.

NIF 6. How did Hulga lose her leg?
Factual. She lost it in a hunting accident.

GO 7. Why does the story begin with a character sketch of Mrs. Freeman?

NC 8. Is O'Connor using Hulga (Joy) Hopewell?
Not clear. What is meant by "using"?

GO 9. Why is Hulga so angry with her mother?

NIF 10. Why does Mrs. Hopewell think young women go to college?
Factual. They look for prospective husbands.

NC 11. If Joy is really a philosopher why is she so rude?
Not clear. The question implies that being a philosopher and being rude are contradictory terms. Not so. What is the question or problem?

NIF 12. Why does Joy look down on young men?
Factual. She thinks she can smell their stupidity.

TOMORROW AND TOMORROW AND SO FORTH
LESSON PLAN 9

1. Focus: Journal writing: Having just completed our reading and discussions of Macbeth, what was your immediate personal reaction to this story about a teacher's efforts to discuss Macbeth's final soliloquy?
(10 minutes)

2. Objective: To solve several questions of interpretation about the overall meaning of the novel.

3. Purpose: To increase our mutual understanding (comprehension) and, as a result, our enjoyment of the story.

4. Input: Begin with a factual quiz to check that everyone has read the novel (Rule 1: No one may participate who has not read the selection). The quiz should be 10 factual questions, short answers (not true/false). Those with 70 percent are in the inner circle; those with less are in the outer circle (15 minutes). Two basic questions (30 or 60 minutes).

5. Modeling, checking, and guided practice: During discussion the coleaders model the four rules of discussion, check for understanding by asking follow-up questions for clarification, substantiation, consistency, relevance, implication, resolution, and to get more opinions. Guided practice is the discussion.

6. Closure: Oral or written resolution of one or two basic questions just discussed.

Note: During Socratic Seminar day(s), in a full 90-minute period, four pairs of student coleaders each lead a 15-minute discussion of the reading. It is important that the teacher approve the student coleader questions before discussion to avoid wasting time on questions that are not clear, are factual, or evaluative. (Discussion should center on solving problems, not in trying to figure out what the problems are.) During the remaining time (if any) the teacher leads a demonstration discussion (modeling) of one of his or her basic questions on the reading of the lesson.

Reading: Updike, John (1978). *Elements of Literature.* Scholes, Robert Ed. New York, Oxford University Press.

BASIC QUESTIONS:
TOMORROW AND TOMORROW AND SO FORTH
BASIC QUESTION OF INTERPRETATION 1

Does Mark Prosser fail to teach his students anything about Macbeth's final soliloquy mainly because he is a weak teacher or because his students are apathetic and resist thinking?

If it is because his students are apathetic, then:

1. Why does Prosser want to know the "exact" meaning of the first two lines of the soliloquy even though he says later "there is no single right answer"? (pp. 55, 58)

2. Does Prosser fear what his students think of him or regard them with contempt? (pp. 54, 59)

3. hy does Prosser mock Peter Forester's interpretation of the opening lines? (p.56)

4. Why does Prosser's admission of fallibility produce "the wrong effect in his class"? (p. 58)

5. Why does Updike portray Prosser as a teacher with a reputation as a talker in class? (p. 57)

6. Why does Prosser try to tell his student's the meaning of the soliloquy? (p. 56)

If it is because Prosser is a weak teacher, then:

7. Is Peter being courteous or confrontational when he asks Mr. Prosser what the passage means? (p. 58)

8. Does Updike want us to believe Prosser when he tells his students that he doesn't have all the answers? (p. 58)

9. Does Prosser believe that he can learn anything from his students? (p. 58)

10. Why does Prosser attempt to soften his own dark interpretation of the soliloquy? (p. 57)

11. Why does Prosser approve of Teresa's interpretation (p. 58) but reject Gloria's? (p. 59)

12. Does Prosser put down Geoffrey Langer because he is smart? (p. 60)

13. Why does Updike end his story with Prosser being duped by Gloria? (pp. 60–63)

14. Does Updike want us to believe that Macbeth's last soliloquy has relevance to Mark Prosser's personal life? (p. 63)

15. When Prosser comments on whether or not Shakespeare is saying that life is a fraud, why does he accept the false assumption in the student's question?

SOME ALTERNATIVE BASIC QUESTIONS

Here are four more basic questions that you can qualify for discussion if you can come up with at least eight related interpretive follow-up questions for each. When students are struggling to write their own basic questions, I sometimes "give" them a basic question as an intermediate step to writing their own clusters. They then have to develop at least eight of their own related interpretive follow-up questions.

BASIC QUESTION OF INTERPRETATION 2

Why is Mark Prosser attracted to Gloria Angstrom?

BASIC QUESTION OF INTERPRETATION 3

Why is Mark Prosser more concerned with getting his students to admire him than with teaching them?

BASIC QUESTION OF INTERPRETATION 4

Why does the author have Mark Prosser learn that Gloria has written a similar love note to other teachers?

PRIDE AND PREJUDICE
LESSON PLAN 10

Six-Day Unit

Lesson 1:   Cast of characters. VHR Chapter 1. Assignments.

Lesson 2:   Plot-check quiz on Volume 1. Clips from VHR of Volume 1.

Lesson 3:   Plot-check quiz on Volume 2. Clips from VHR of Volume 2.

Lesson 4:   Plot-check quiz on Volume 3. Clips from VHR of Volume 4.

Lesson 5:   Seminar: three basic questions.

Lesson 6:   Essay Exam and Answer Key.

1.	Focus:	*Journal writing:* Copy the first sentence of the novel and then paraphrase it. Write a one-page commentary on whether or not Jane Austen's observation applies to today's world.
2.	Objective:	To solve several questions of interpretation about the overall meaning of the novel.
3.	Purpose:	To increase our mutual understanding (comprehension) and, as a result, our enjoyment of the story.
4.	Input:	Begin with a factual quiz on each Volume (1–3) to check that everyone has read the novel (Rule 1: No one may participate who has not read the selection). Three basic questions. (30 or 60 minutes)
5.	Modeling, checking, and guided practice:	During discussion the coleaders *model* the four rules of discussion, *check for understanding* by asking follow-up questions for clarification, substantiation, consistency, relevance, implication, resolution, and to get more opinion. *Guided practice* IS the discussion.
6.	Closure:	Oral or written resolution of one or two basic questions just discussed.

Note: During Socratic Seminar day(s), in a full 90-minute period, four pairs of student coleaders each lead a 15-minute discussion of the reading. It is important that the teacher approves the student coleader questions before discussion to avoid wasting time on questions that are not clear, are factual, or evaluative. (Discussion should center on solving problems, not in trying to figure out what the problems are.) During the remaining time (if any) the teacher leads a demonstration discussion (modeling) of one of his or her basic questions on the reading of the lesson.

Reading: Austen, Jane. *Pride and Prejudice.* New York, Bantam, 1981.

PRIDE AND PREJUDICE:
LESSON 1—CAST OF CHARACTERS & ASSIGNMENTS

CAST OF CHARACTERS

◆ *Mr. and Mrs. Bennet:* parents of five unique daughters. "The business of her [Mrs. Bennet's] life was to get her daughters married" that is, "to make a good establishment" (to marry into wealth).

  • *Elizabeth (Lizzy) Bennet*: heroine, intelligent, spirited, independent, realistic, opinionated, perceptive, prejudiced, and prideful.

  • *Jane Bennet:* the oldest daughter, gentle and serene, she looks for the best in everyone.

  • *Mary Bennet:* third daughter, superficial and pretentious, she tries to make up for her lack of natural beauty with a pedantic display of learning.

  • *Catherine (Kitty) Bennet:* a peevish soldier-chasing daughter, superficial like Lydia.

  • *Lydia Bennet:* the youngest daughter, giddy, stupid, naive, and vulnerable. Mrs. Bennet's favorite.

  • *Mr. Collins* ["Mr. Manners"]: Mr. Bennet's cousin, an ingratiating clergyman who will inherit Longbourn at Mr. Bennet's death since he has no male heir.

  • *Mr. and Mrs. Gardener:* Mrs. Bennet's intelligent and cultivated brother and sister-in-law.

  • *Mr. and Mrs. Phillips:* a county attorney and his vulgar wife who is the sister of Mrs. Bennet.

◆ *Mr. Charles Bingley*: he rents nearby Netherfield. Genial and upright. Falls in love with Jane.

  • *Caroline Bingley:* cold, selfish sister of Charles who is determined to marry Mr. Darcy.

  • *Mr. and Mrs. Hurst:* Bingley's snobbish sister and apathetic brother-in-law.

◆ *Fitzwilliam Darcy:* snobbish, rich, arrogant, condescending, a personification of pride and prejudice. Charles Bingley's unlikely friend. He has ambivalent feelings about Elizabeth.

  • *Georgiana Darcy:* Darcy's shy but good and warm-hearted sister.

  • *Colonel Fitzwilliam:* Darcy's genial cousin who is infatuated with Elizabeth.

  • *Lady Catherine de Bourgh:* Darcy's insolent aunt.

  • *Miss de Bourgh [Anne]:* Lady Catherine's insipid, near invalid daughter.

◆ *Sir William and Lady Lucas:* the Bennet's neighbors and Charlotte's parents.

  • *Charlotte Lucas:* Elizabeth's confidant and equally intelligent friend who disappoints Elizabeth when she marries Mr. Collins for his wealth.

♦ *George Wickam:* a handsome, personable, but unprincipled man who elopes with Lydia. He goes out of his way to defame Darcy's character to get revenge for supposed wrongs.

ASSIGNMENTS

♦ *Exercise 1:   Vocabulary:* Circle in red any unfamiliar words. Make up a list of these words along with a page number for each. Review in context.

♦ *Exercise 2:*   Cite and explain *five specific examples of irony* (verbal or dramatic) in Volume 1 of Jane Austen's *Pride and Prejudice—First Impressions.*

♦ *Exercise 3:*   Film version and *movie reviews.* Read the movie reviews of *Pride and Prejudice* at Amazon.com. Select one review that you strongly agree *or* disagree with and write a one-page response or commentary. Option: publish your own review of the novel on Amazon.com.

♦ *Exercise 4:   Basic questions for discussion.* Write at least eight specific follow-up questions for these problems of interpretation. Include a page reference for each question.

(A) Does Jane Austen want us to conclude that the phrase "pride and prejudice" *applies equally* to Elizabeth as well as to Darcy? Example: Why does Elizabeth point out similarities between herself and Darcy? (p. 69)

(B) How would Austen have her readers explain why Elizabeth falls in love with someone like Darcy? Examples: Why is Elizabeth so eager to distrust Mr. Darcy at the outset of the novel, but disposed to trust Mr. Wickham? (pp. 57–62) Why does Elizabeth want to avoid her parents' kind of marriage? (pp. 176–177)

♦ *Exercise 5.   Essay options.* Write a well organized essay that develops one of the topics or questions below.

(A) Why does Jane Austen resort to dramatic and verbal irony so often in her story? Cite and explain at least two specific examples of each. Do not bother with an introduction; begin with the thesis. Conclude by answering the question.

(B) Cite and explain *two specific examples of irony* (verbal and dramatic) in Volumes 2 and 3 of Jane Austen's *Pride and Prejudice—First Impressions.*

(C) In what sense is Jane Austen's novel *antiromantic*? What are the major elements or characteristics of romanticism? Which of these does Austen reject or down play?

(D) What *value or dominant character trait* does each of the five Bennet daughters represent or embody? Jane? Elizabeth? Mary? Catherine? Lydia?

♦ *Exercise 6*: Take a review quiz on each of the three volumes of *Pride and Prejudice.*

♦ *Exercise 7*: Check out *Jane Austen's Web site:* http://www.ee.ulberta.ca/~dawe/ austen.html Write a report on what you found that was of interest to you or that helped you in your reading and interpretation of *Pride and Prejudice.*

PRIDE AND PREJUDICE:
LESSON 2—REVIEW QUIZ

Volume One [1–23]

Directions: Answer each question in the space beneath it in a brief sentence or two.

1. What does the first sentence of the novel mean: "It is a truth universally acknowledged, that a single man in possession of a good fortune must be in want of a wife."

2. Why is Mrs. Bennet so determined and anxious to get her five daughters married?

3. How does Mr. Bennet demonstrate that he is sensitive to his wife's feelings about their daughters?

4. Why does Mr. Bingley's arrival at Netherfield arouse Mrs. Bennett's immediate interest?

5. What is the apparent chief difference between the personalities of Mr. Bingley and Mr. Darcy?

6. Why does Darcy refuse to dance with Elizabeth at the (first) ball at Meryton?

7. When Elizabeth visits Charlotte Lucas what does Charlotte say about Jane Bennet?

8. Early in the novel, how does Austen illustrate the pride and prejudice in Elizabeth?

9. Early in the novel, how does Austen illustrate the pride and prejudice in Mr. Darcy?

10. What is the major difference between Charlotte's view of marriage and that of Elizabeth and Jane?

11. Why does Austen remind us that Longbourn would go to Mr. Collins on Mr. Bennet's death?

12. After reading Mr. Collins' long, self-serving letter, why does Mr. Bennet welcome his visit to his home?

13. According to Elizabeth, what "defect of character" makes Darcy blind to the good qualities of others?

14. According to Darcy, what "defect of character" makes Elizabeth blind to the good qualities of others?

15. Why is Elizabeth able to discern Mr. Collins' true character but not Mr. Darcy's?

16. How does Mr. Wickham make Elizabeth even more set in her low opinion of Mr. Darcy?

17. What is Jane's reaction to Elizabeth's low opinion of Mr. Darcy?

18. What is one of Mr. Collins three reasons for proposing marriage to Elizabeth?

19. Why is Elizabeth so turned off by Mr. Collins' marriage proposal?

20. Why is Elizabeth so disappointed in Charlotte's marriage to Mr. Collins?

SCORE: 20 × 5 = 100

PRIDE AND PREJUDICE:
REVIEW QUIZ—ANSWER KEY

Volume One [1–23]

Directions: Answer each question in the space beneath it in a brief sentence or two.

1. What does the first sentence of the novel mean: "It is a truth universally acknowledged, that a single man in possession of a good fortune must be in want of a wife."

    One of the most famous sentences in English literature is a masterpiece of irony that sets the tone for the entire novel—pretentious and yet banal. The "truth" of the sentence is that a wealthy man must need a wife, but in reality it is the woman without a fortune that needs a man with a fortune for a husband.

2. Why is Mrs. Bennet so determined and anxious to get her five daughters married?

    Mr. Bennet has no male heir to pass on his estate to. By English law at the time, an estate cannot be inherited by a female. Mr. Collins happens to be the next male in line—something about which he is all too conscious.

3. How does Mr. Bennet demonstrate that he is sensitive to his wife's feelings about their daughters?

    He visits their new wealthy neighbor, Mr. Bingley even though he pretends indifference.

4. Why does Mr. Bingley's arrival at Netherfield arouse Mrs. Bennett's immediate interest?

    He is a wealthy, eligible bachelor who is also out-going and friendly.

5. What is the apparent chief difference between the personalities of Mr. Bingley and Mr. Darcy?

    While Bingley is affable and gregarious, Mr. Darcy is aloof, reserved, and arrogant.

6. Why does Darcy refuse to dance with Elizabeth at the (first) ball at Meryton?

    He says that she is "not handsome enough to tempt him."

7. When Elizabeth visits Charlotte Lucas what does Charlotte say about Jane Bennet?

She defends Jane's interest in Bingley even though she knows next-to-nothing about him. Charlotte believes that a marriage is better when the partners do not know each other well.

8. Early in the novel, how does Austen illustrate the pride and prejudice in Elizabeth?

    Elizabeth's pride blinds her from seeing any potential good in Mr. Darcy.

9. Early in the novel, how does Austen illustrate the pride and prejudice in Mr. Darcy?

    Because he is particularly conscious of his social status, Mr. Darcy treats most beneath him with condescension.

10. What is the major difference between Charlotte's view of marriage and that of Elizabeth and Jane?

    Charlotte is no romantic; she is resigned to marrying for convenience, position, and practicality. Elizabeth and Jane are romantics who will marry for no less than love; however, they are also conscious of the importance of social position.

11. Why does Austen remind us that Longbourn would go to Mr. Collins on Mr. Bennet's death?

    Austin reminds us of English law that Mr. Bennet's estate can be inherited only by a male heir. This unfair situation explains Mrs. Bennet's obsession to have each of her daughters "make a good establishment" (marry into wealth).

12. After reading Mr. Collins' long, self-serving letter, why does Mr. Bennet welcome his visit to his home?

    He looks forward to some entertainment: watching Mr. Collins grovel.

13. According to Elizabeth, what "defect of character" makes Darcy blind to the good qualities of others?

    "Your defect is a propensity to hate everybody."

14. According to Darcy, what "defect of character" makes Elizabeth blind to the good qualities of others?

    "And yours. . . is willfully to misunderstand them."

15. Why is Elizabeth able to discern Mr. Collins' true character but not Mr. Darcy's?

She sees that Collins is not a sensible man because she has no personal interest in him. Her pride blinds her to Darcy's good qualities because she may have a subconscious interest in him.

16. How does Mr. Wickham make Elizabeth even more set in her low opinion of Mr. Darcy?

He tells her how badly Darcy had treated him and she readily believes him.

17. What is Jane's reaction to Elizabeth's low opinion of Mr. Darcy?

Characteristically, she defends both Wickham and Darcy; she cannot believe that Bingley is so deceived by Darcy nor can she imagine that someone so amiable as Wickham can lie.

18. What is one of Mr. Collins three reasons for proposing marriage to Elizabeth?

- As a clergyman, he believes that he should "set the example" of matrimony in his parish.

- He believes that marriage would greatly add to his happiness.

- Lady Catherine has advised him that he should be married.

19. Why is Elizabeth so turned off by Mr. Collins' marriage proposal?

Entirely self serving and presumptuous, Collins cannot believe that Elizabeth would refuse him.

20. Why is Elizabeth so disappointed in Charlotte's marriage to Mr. Collins?

She married not for love but for security, convenience, social position, and wealth.

SCORE: 20 × 5 = 100

PRIDE AND PREJUDICE:
LESSON 3—REVIEW QUIZ

Volume Two [24–42]

Directions: Answer each question in the space beneath it in a brief sentence or two.

1.   Why does Jane go to London with Mr. and Mrs. Gardener?

2. Why does Mr. Gardener caution Elizabeth about Wickham?

3.   Why does Jane try to get in touch with Caroline Bingley when she is in London?

4.   How does Caroline Bingley treat Jane in London? Why?

5.   When Elizabeth visits Charlotte (now Mrs. Collins), how does Mr. Collins treat Elizabeth?

6.   During her visit, what does Elizabeth think now of Charlotte's marriage to Mr. Collins?

7.   What is Elizabeth's estimation of Lady Catherine de Bourgh's character?

8.   Why was Lady Catherine offended by Elizabeth's manner?

9.   Why does Lady Catherine rudely evaluate Elizabeth's taste in music and skill at the piano?

10. Although Colonel Fitzwilliam openly admires Elizabeth, why is he unable to marry her?

11. How does Elizabeth learn that Darcy was instrumental in making Bingley forget Jane?

12. Why does Elizabeth reject Darcy's marriage proposal?

13. Why was Darcy opposed to Bingley and Jane's relationship?

14. What was the purpose of Darcy's long letter to Elizabeth?

15. How does Elizabeth react at first to Darcy's letter?

16. What makes Elizabeth eventually change her mind about Darcy's letter?

17. What does Elizabeth learn about herself after reconsidering Darcy's letter?

18. Why does Elizabeth tell her father not to allow Lydia to go to Brighton for the summer?

19. Why is Elizabeth so eager to accompany Mr. and Mrs. Gardener during their vacation?

20. Under what condition does Elizabeth agree to accompany the Gardiner's visit to Pemberley?

SCORE: 20 × 5 = 100

PRIDE AND PREJUDICE:
REVIEW QUIZ—ANSWER KEY

Volume Two [24–42]

Directions: Answer each question in the space beneath it in a brief sentence or two.

1. Why does Jane go to London with Mr. and Mrs. Gardener?

    She hopes to develop her relationship with Bingley.

2. Why does Mrs. Gardener caution Elizabeth about Wickham?

    She ought not to fall in love with someone without money.

3. Why does Jane try to get in touch with Caroline Bingley when she is in London?

    She hopes that she will tell her brother that she is in town.

4. How does Caroline Bingley treat Jane? Why?

    Caroline is aloof and cold. She tells Jane that her brother *knows* that she is in town. At this point, even Jane begins to perceive Caroline's insincerity and deception.

5. When Elizabeth visits Charlotte (now Mrs. Collins), how does Mr. Collins treat Elizabeth?

    He goes out of his way to show her what she has missed in rejecting his marriage proposal.

6. During her visit, what does Elizabeth's think now of Charlotte's marriage to Mr. Collins?

    She notices that Charlotte is reasonably happy and comfortable with Mr. Collins. She also notes that Charlotte has taken on Mr. Collins need to be in Lady Catherine's favor.

7. What is Elizabeth's estimation of Lady Catherine de Bourgh's character?

    She regards her as an insolent, arrogant aristocrat who is condescending, ill-bred, and fond of making self-serving statements.

8. Why was Lady Catherine offended by Elizabeth's manner?

    Elizabeth speaks her mind forthrightly with out any pretension.

9. Why does Lady Catherine rudely evaluate Elizabeth's taste in music and skill at the piano?

    Elizabeth upstages Lady Catherine when she plays the piano for Colonel Fitzwilliam and draws Mr. Darcy away from his conversation with Lady Catherine.

10. Although Colonel Fitzwilliam openly admires Elizabeth, why is he unable to marry her?

    As a younger son, he will inherit no property.

11. How does Elizabeth learn that Darcy was instrumental in making Bingley forget Jane?

    Colonel Fitzwilliam inadvertently tells her.

12. Why does Elizabeth reject Darcy's marriage proposal?

    She condemns him for separating Jane and Bingley, for treating Wickham viciously, and for his arrogance and selfishness.

13. Why was Darcy opposed to Bingley and Jane's relationship?

    He believed that because Jane was somewhat withdrawn by nature, her love for Bingley could not be genuine. He wanted to save his friend from a mediocre marriage.

14. What was the purpose of Darcy's long letter to Elizabeth?

    He wanted to defend himself and explain to her without passion and honestly that he had acted out of sincere concern for Jane and Bingley. He also revealed the true nature of Wickham.

15. How does Elizabeth react at first to Darcy's letter?

    She reads the letter "with a strong prejudice against every thing he might say." As a result, she at first refuses to believe Darcy thinking that he is neither honest nor sincere.

16. What makes Elizabeth eventually change her mind about Darcy's letter?

    She reconsiders the evidence: Wickham's actions were often inconsistent while Darcy, in her presence, had never done anything not honorable and just. Once she accepted one statement as true, she then realizes that she must accept every fact as true or reject them all as false.

17. What does Elizabeth learn about her self after reconsidering Darcy's letter?

   Her own pride and prejudice had blinded her to Darcy's true character. To her own shock and chagrin, she realizes how despicably and unfairly she had acted in condemning Darcy so severely and without a fair trial. She says, "Had I been in love, I could not have been more wretchedly blind. But vanity not love, has been my folly.…Till this moment I never knew myself.

18. Why does Elizabeth tell her father not to allow Lydia to go to Brighton for the summer?

   Since she now is convinced that Wickham is indeed a man of no principle, she fears that naive Lydia could be easily duped by him if she went to Brighton where he would be stationed.

19. Why is Elizabeth so eager to accompany Mr. and Mrs. Gardener during their vacation?

   She is so devastated and depressed by what she had done to Darcy and may have evenruined her relationship beyond repair, she looked forward to a complete change of scene.

20. Under what condition does Elizabeth agree to accompany the Gardiner's visit to Pemberley?

   She had to be reassured that Darcy would not be present.

SCORE: 20 × 5 = 100

PRIDE AND PREJUDICE:
LESSON 4—REVIEW QUIZ

Volume Three [43–60]

Directions: Answer each question in the space beneath it in a brief sentence or two.

1. What does Elizabeth learn about Darcy from his housekeeper that puzzles her?

2. Why does this information make Elizabeth feel guilty as well as somewhat despondent?

3. How does Darcy react when he suddenly and unexpectedly meets Elizabeth at Pemberley?

4. How does Miss Bingley display her jealousy of Elizabeth?

5. What causes Darcy to say that Elizabeth is one of the handsomest women of his acquaintance?

6. Why is Elizabeth so upset by the two letters that she receives from Jane?

7. How does Darcy react to the news of Elizabeth's predicament?

8. At this moment, why does Elizabeth now realize that she loves Darcy?

9. What is ironic about her realization at this time?

10. Why is Elizabeth sure that Wickham will not marry Lydia?

11. What conditions does Mr. Bennet agree to so that Wickham will marry his daughter?

12. Who does Mr. Bennet believe helped him to meet Wickham's conditions?

13. When Mr. and Mrs. Wickham arrive at Longbourn, how do Mr. and Mrs. Bennet receive them?

14. Who in fact enabled Mr. Bennet to meet Mr. Wickham's conditions?

15. When Bingley proposes to Jane, what does he finally learn about their relationship?

16. Why does Lady Catherine suddenly appear at Longbourn?

17. At this point, what ironically causes Elizabeth and Darcy to declare their mutual love for one another?

18. What is so ironic about Mr. Bennet's initial objection to Elizabeth's marrying Darcy?

19. What is the difference between Jane's love for Bingley and Elizabeth's love for Darcy?

20. What caused Georgiana to be astonished and even alarmed at Elizabeth's treatment of her brother?

SCORE: 20 × 5 = 100

PRIDE AND PREJUDICE:
REVIEW QUIZ—ANSWER Key

Volume Three [43–60]

Directions: Answer each question in the space beneath it in a brief sentence or two.

1. What does Elizabeth learn about Darcy from his housekeeper that puzzles her?

   She praises the virtues of her master as a compassionate, patient, caring person. Although some may think him arrogant, *she* has never seen any of it. Indeed, she has never heard him speak a cross word.

2. Why does this information make Elizabeth feel guilty as well as somewhat despondent?

   Elizabeth now has more evidence that she has been blind to Darcy's good qualities. She also thinks momentarily that *she* could have been mistress of such a magnificent estate.

3. How does Darcy react when he suddenly and unexpectedly meets Elizabeth at Pemberley?

   He is extremely friendly and attentive—more than he has ever been before. Elizabeth is particularly pleased that she can introduce him to the Gardiners (class people) and that he wants to introduce her to his sister.

4. How does Miss Bingley display her jealousy of Elizabeth?

   She insults her indirectly by referring to Wickham's elopement with Lydia. She even begins speaking despairingly of Elizabeth's appearance and clothes.

5. What causes Darcy to say that Elizabeth is one of the handsomest women of his acquaintance?

   When Miss Bingley speaks despairingly of Elizabeth's appearance and clothes, Darcy defends Elizabeth.

6. Why is Elizabeth so upset by the two letters that she receives from Jane?

   She learned that Lydia had eloped with Wickham and may not get married. This shame on her family meant the end of any hope of a marriage to Darcy.

7. How does Darcy react to the news of Elizabeth's predicament?

He comes to the inn in London and is truly concerned when he hears what has happened. He feels his own silence regarding Wickham is, in part, responsible. Thinking that he is but an intruder, Darcy leaves.

8. At this moment, why does Elizabeth now realize that she loves Darcy?

Darcy's concern and compassion is genuine *and* he gave no thought to anyone's social status. He is determined to help resolve Lydia's unfortunate circumstances.

9. What is ironic about her realization at this time?

Elizabeth realizes that she loves Darcy just when she fears that a family scandal will ruin her chances forever.

10. Why is Elizabeth sure that Wickham will not marry Lydia?

Elizabeth knows Wickham would not marry Lydia because she will inherit no real wealth.

11. What conditions does Mr. Bennet agree to so that Wickham will marry his daughter?

Wickham's gambling debts must be paid and he and Lydia will be given a yearly stipend.

12. Who does Mr. Bennet believe helped him to meet Wickham's conditions?

He believes that Mr. Gardener must have spent a lot of his own money.

13. When Mr. and Mrs. Wickham arrive at Longbourn, how do Mr. and Mrs. Bennet receive them?

Mrs. Bennet seems proud of the way the marriage came about and regrets that they will be living so far away. Mr. Bennet refuses to admit them to his house until Jane and Elizabeth convince him to do so for Lydia's sake.

14. Who in fact enabled Mr. Bennet to meet Mr. Wickham's conditions?

Mrs. Gardener writes to inform Elizabeth that it was Darcy, not her husband, who found Lydia and Wickham and then persuaded Wickham to marry Lydia with s substantial marriage settlement. Wickham's debts were paid, his wife would receive a thousand pounds in addition to her one thousand pound marriage portion and small yearly stipend—and he was bought a commission in the army.

15. When Bingley proposes to Jane, what does he finally learn about their relationship?

    He discovers that Jane had been in London and he left only because he thought that Jane no longer cared for him. His sister had undermined their relationship.

16. Why does Lady Catherine suddenly appear at Longbourn?

    She demands that Elizabeth assure her that she has no plans whatever to marry Darcy since he and Miss de Bough had been intended for each other from the cradle.

17. At this point, what ironically causes Elizabeth and Darcy to declare their mutual love for one another?

    When they both discover that Lady Catherine had tried to crush their relationship, and that they had both maintained their independence and refused to be intimidated, Darcy again asks Elizabeth to marry him.

18. What is so ironic about Mr. Bennet's initial objection to Elizabeth's marrying Darcy?

    He begs his daughter not to marry someone she cannot respect—the very mistake that *he* had made in marrying his wife.

19. What is the difference between Jane's love for Bingley and Elizabeth's love for Darcy?

    Jane feels that she is in love but Elizabeth knows and feels that she is in love.

20. What caused Georgiana to be astonished and even alarmed at Elizabeth's treatment of her brother?

    Elizabeth speaks up to her husband as an equal and even points out his faults.

SCORE: 20 × 5 = 100

PRIDE AND PREJUDICE:
LESSON 5—SEMINAR

Note: We will have three 20-minute discussions lead by coleaders on three basic questions. Each pair of coleaders will prepare 10 interpretive follow-up questions for their chosen or assigned basic question. Those not leading a discussion will prepare five interpretive follow-up questions for two of the three basic questions that follow. Be sure to include a page reference for each follow-up question.

BASIC QUESTION OF INTERPRETATION 1

Does Jane Austen want us to conclude that the phrase "pride and prejudice" applies equally to Elizabeth as well as to Mr. Darcy?

BASIC QUESTION OF INTERPRETATION 2

How would Jane Austen have us explain Elizabeth falling in love with Mr. Darcy?

BASIC QUESTION OF INTERPRETATION 3

According to Jane Austen, what is the difference between a good marriage and a merely tolerable one?

PRIDE AND PREJUDICE:
LESSON 6—ESSAY EXAM

[_____/200]   Name_____ (print)

Directions: First, in the space beneath each quotation, identify the speaker or speakers (*who*) and the event (*when*) in the novel. Second, on the paper provided, write a full half-page commentary on *four* quotations. In each commentary: (1) identify the speaker or speakers (*who*) of the quotation; (2) explain its context (*when*) and overall content (*what*); and then (3) explain how its *tone* is integral to its *theme*. *Note:* Do not copy the quotation, do not skip lines, and use ink.

SCORE: Quotations: $12 + 13 = 15 \times 13 = 195 + 5 = 200$
              Commentaries: $10 + 15 = 25 \times 8 = 200$

EXAMPLE

16. "I feel it my duty to promote the blessing of peace in all families within reach of my influence; and on these grounds I flatter myself that my present overtures of goodwill are highly commendable, and that the circumstance of my being next in the entail of Longbourn estate will kindly be overlooked on your side, and not lead you to reject the offered olive branch. I cannot be otherwise than concerned at being the means of injuring your amiable daughters, and beg leave to apologize for it, as well as to assure you of my readiness to make every possible amends." (p. 47)

Who: _Mr. Collins_   When:_His first letter to Mr. Bennet just after the arrival_
                          of Mr. Bingley

COMMENTARY NO. 16:
MR. MANNERS' CONCERN

During his long letter to Mr. Bennet after the arrival and stir caused by Mr. Bingley among Mrs.Bennet and her daughters, Mr. Collins (Mr. Manners) writes a long self-serving message to Mr. Bennet ostensibly to apologize for being heir to Longbourn on his death but his real intent is to suggest that he and Mrs. Bennet need not be concerned because he would be willing to marry one of their daughters. The pretentious and obsequious tone of his letter clashes with Jane Austen's tone of irony and antipathy: irony because none of the Bennet girls would marry a man who thinks he is such "a catch" and antipathy because Collins' pathetic fawning. As a result the theme here is clear: can love be separated in marriage from fortune and security?

QUOTATIONS

[_____/200]

1. "It is a truth universally acknowledged that a single man in possession of a good fortune must be in want of a wife."

Speaker(s)_____ When:_____

2. "Happiness in marriage is entirely a matter of chance. If the dispositions of the parties are ever so well known to each other…it does not advance their felicity in the least. They always continue to grow sufficiently unlike afterwards to have their share of vexation, and it is better to know as little as possible of the defects of the person with whom you are to pass your life."

Speaker(s)_____ When:_____

3. "There is, I believe, in every disposition a tendency to some particular evil, a natural defect, which not even the best education can overcome." 'And your defect is a propensity to hate everybody.' 'And yours…is willfully to misunderstand them.'"

Speaker(s)_____ When:_____

4. "I have known him too well and too long to be a fair judge. It is impossible for me to be impartial…He is not at all liked. Everybody is disgusted with his pride…The world is blinded by his fortune and consequence, or frightened by his high and imposing manners. …His behavior to myself has been scandalous…his late father bequeathed me of the best living in his gift…and meant to provide for me amply, and thought he had done it; but when the living fell, it was given elsewhere. "'Good heavens! but how could that be?—How could his will be disregarded?' 'A man of honor could not have doubted the intention of my godfather, but M. chose to doubt it.'"

Speaker(s)_____ When:_____

5. "'Almost as soon as I entered the house I singled you out as the companion of my future life. But before I am run away with by my feelings…perhaps it will be advisable for me to state my reasons for

marrying…first, that I think it a right thing for every clergyman in easy circumstance to set the example….Secondly, that I am convinced it will add very greatly to my happiness; and thirdly, which perhaps I ought to have mentioned earlier, that it is the particular advice and recommendation of a very noble lady whom I call patroness.'…'You are too hasty sir…you forget that I have made no reply.'"

Speaker(s)_____ When:_____

6. "Why should you be surprised. Do you think in incredible that Mr. Collins should be able to procure any woman's good opinion, because he was not so happy as to succeed with you?…I see you must be very much surprised….But when you have had time to think if over, I hope you will be satisfied with what I have done. I am no romantic, you know. I never was. I ask only a comfortable home…and I am convinced that my chance of happiness with him is as fair as most people can boast on entering marriage."

Speaker(s)_____ When:_____

7. "She could not be insensible to the compliment of such a man's affection…she was at first sorry for the pain he was to receive. . .He *spoke* of apprehension and anxiety, but his countenance expressed real security.'…'I have never desired your good opinion…do you think that any consideration would tempt me to accept the man who has been the means of ruining, perhaps forever, the happiness of a most beloved sister?'"

Speaker(s)_____ When:_____

8. "Her father…had married a woman whose weak understanding and illiberal mind had very early in their marriage put an end of all real affection for her. Respect, esteem, and confidence had vanished forever. . .To his wife he was very little indebted than as her ignorance and folly had contributed to his amusement. This was not the sort of happiness which a man would in general owe to his wife. …Elizabeth, however, had never been blind to the impropriety of her father's behavior as a husband…grateful for his affectionate treatment of herself, she endeavored to forget what she could not

overlook…in exposing his wife to the contempt of her own children was still so highly reprehensible."

Speaker(s)_____ When:_____

9. "This is a most unfortunate affair; and will probably be much talked of. But we must stem the tide of malice, and pour into the wounded bosoms of each other the balm of sisterly consolation…Unhappy as the event must be for my sister, we may draw from it this useful lesson: loss of virtue in a female is irretrievable…and that she cannot be too much guarded in her behavior towards the undeserving of the other sex."

Speaker(s)_____ When:_____

10. "Only think of its being three months since I went away…Good gracious! When I went away, I am sure I had no more idea of being married till I came back again! though I thought it would be very good fun if I was….What do you think of my husband? Is not he a charming man? I am sure my sisters must all envy me. I only hope they may have half my good luck. They must all go to Brighton. That is the place to get husbands. What a pity it is…we did not all go."

Speaker(s)_____ When:_____

11. "He has made me so happy by telling me that he was totally ignorant of my being in town last spring! I had not believed it possible…I am certainly the most fortunate creature that ever existed! …Why am I thus singled from my family and blessed above them all! If I could but see you as happy, dear sister! If there *were* but such another man for you!"

Speaker(s)_____ When:_____

12. "Has he made you an offer of marriage?…Do you know who I am?…He is engaged to *my daughter*. Now what have you to say? …Will you promise me never to enter into an engagement? 'I will make no promise of the kind.' 'I shall not go away until you have given me the assurance I require.' 'And I certainly *never* shall give it…I am not to be intimidated…You have widely mistaken my character if you think I can be worked on by such persuasions as these.'"

Speaker(s)_____ When:_____

13. "If your feelings are still what they were last April, tell me so at once. My affections and wishes are unchanged, but one word from you will silence me forever...You showed me how insufficient were all my pretensions to please a woman worthy of being pleased...I am almost afraid of asking what you thought of me when we met at Pemberley. Did you blame me for coming?'"

Speaker(s)_____ When:_____

14. "I am quite sorry that you should be forced to have that disagreeable man all to yourself...Are you out of your senses, to be accepting this man? Have you not always hated him?...Good gracious! Lord bless me! Mr. Darcy!...How rich and great you will be!...Such a charming man!'"

Speaker(s)_____ When:_____

15. "Pemberley was not Georgiana's home; and the attachment of the sisters was exactly what Darcy had hoped to see. They were able to love each other, even as well as they intended. She had the highest opinion in the world of Elizabeth; though at first she often listened with astonishment bordering on alarm at her lively, sportive manner of talking to her brother."

Speaker(s)_____ When:_____

PRIDE AND PREJUDICE:
ESSAY EXAM—ANSWER KEY

[_____/200]   Name_____ (print)

Directions: First, in the space beneath each quotation, identify the speaker or speakers (*who*) and the event (*when*) in the novel. Second, on the paper provided, write a full half-page commentary on *four* quotations. In each commentary: (1) identify the speaker or speakers (*who*) of the quotation; (2) explain its context (*when*) and overall content (*what*), and then (3) explain how its *tone* is integral to its *theme*. *Note:* Do not copy the quotation, do not skip lines, and use ink.

SCORE: Quotations: $12 + 13 = 15 \times 13 = 195 + 5 = 200$
Commentaries: $10 + 15 = 25 \times 8 = 200$

QUOTATIONS
[_____/200]

1. *Speaker(s)* narrator   *When:* the first sentence of the novel (p. 1).

2. *Speaker(s)* Charlotte   *When:* she tells Elizabeth that Jane could just as well marry Bingley now as wait to get to know him better (p. 16)

3. *Speaker(s)* Darcy/ Eliza   *When:* during a conversation after another Meryton ball (p. 43)

4. *Speaker(s)* Wickham/ Elizabeth   *When:* at a Meryton ball when Wickham defames Darcy's character (60)

5. *Speaker(s)* Collins/ Eliza   *When:* after a second visit to her home—Longbourn (p. 80).

6. *Speaker(s)* Charlotte/ Eliza   *When:* after she accepts Mr. Collins' offer of marriage (p. 95)

7. *Speaker(s)* narrator/ Elizabeth   *When:* she rejects Darcy's first marriage proposal (p. 143)

8. *Speaker(s)* narrator   *When:* Jane and Elizabeth discuss their parents' marriage (pp. 176–177)

9. *Speaker(s)* Mary   *When:* Lydia elopes with Wickham and shames the family name (p. 215)

10. *Speaker(s)* Lydia   *When:* she triumphantly returns home to show off Wickham (pp. 235–236)

11. *Speaker(s)* Jane   *When:* she tells Elizabeth of her deep love for Bingley (p. 262)

12. *Speaker(s)* Lady Catherine/Eliza   *When:* she demands that Elizabeth reject Darcy (p. 265)

13. *Speaker(s)* Darcy/Eliza   *When:* Darcy proposes marriage to Elizabeth a second time (p. 274)

14. *Speaker(s)* Mrs. Bennet   *When:* before and after Mrs. Bennet learns of the engagement of Darcy and Elizabeth (pp. 281–284)

15. *Speaker(s)* narrator   *When:* the conclusion of the novel, the "summing up" (p. 291).

THE METAMORPHOSIS
LESSON PLAN 11

1. Focus: Do you know anyone whose entire normal life has been entirely changed in a moment to one of complete dependence?

2. Objective: To solve several questions of interpretation about the overall meaning of the novel.

3. Purpose: To increase our mutual understanding (comprehension) and, as a result, our enjoyment of the story.

4. Input: Begin with a factual quiz to check that everyone has read the novel (Rule 1: No one may participate who has not read the selection). The quiz should be 10 factual questions, short answers (not true/false). Those with 70% are in the inner circle; those with less are in the outer circle (15 minutes). Two or four basic questions (30 or 60 minutes).

5. Modeling, checking, and guided practice: During discussion the coleaders *model* the four rules of discussion, *check for understanding* by asking follow-up questions for clarification, substantiation, consistency, relevance, implication, resolution, and to get more opinions. *Guided practice* IS the discussion.

6. Closure: Oral or written resolution of one or two basic questions just discussed.

Note: During Socratic Seminar day(s), in a full 90-minute period, four pairs of student coleaders each lead a 15-minute discussion of the reading. It is important that the teacher approves the student coleader questions before discussion to avoid wasting time on questions that are not clear, factual, or evaluative. (Discussion should center on solving problems, not in trying to figure out what the problems are.) During the remaining time (if any) the teacher leads a demonstration discussion (modeling) of one of his or her basic questions on the reading of the lesson.

Reading: Kafka, Franz (1972) *The Metamorphosis.* New York, Bantam Books.

METAMORPHOSIS
BASIC QUESTIONS

BASIC INTERPRETIVE QUESTION 1

According to Kafka, has Gregor or his family undergone the greater metamorphosis?

If Gregor has, then:

1. Why does Gregor's father resume his role as head of the family? (pp. 37, 41, 56)

2. Why does Gregor's ailing mother begin to make money selling lingerie to supplement the family's income? (p. 40)

3. Why does Grete become a salesgirl to support the family (p. 41) and take the initiative to solve the family's dilemma about what to do with Gregor? (p. 51)

4. Why is Grete is the only family member who believes that the metamorphosed Gregor is still her brother and tries to care for his needs as long as she can? (pp. 21–25)

5. Why does the story end with the family looking forward to their future prospects: moving to another apartment, taking a trip to the country, and Grete blossoming into a beautiful young woman? (pp. 57–58)

If his family has, then:

6. Why does Gregor overcome his extreme dislike for his job that he kept only to support his family and now feels shame and guilt because his family can no longer rely on him? (pp. 4, 29)

7. Why does Gregor risk leaving his room to let his sister know how deeply her playing the violin moved him and reasserts his determination to send his sister to the Conservatory to study violin? (pp. 27, 49)

8. Since Gregor's "greatest pride" was his consideration for the feelings of others, why does he go out of his way to hide his repulsive body from his family whenever possible? (p. 48)

9. Why does the narrator say that Gregor's conviction to unburden his family by leaving it is greater than his sister's desire to remove him? (p. 54)

10. As his final act of love for his family, why does Gregory starve is himself to death so he will no longer be a burden to them? (pp. 43, 45, 47, 51, 55)

11. Why did Gregor did not become bitter over his father's violent, hateful rejections?

SOME ALTERNATIVE BASIC QUESTIONS

Here are three more basic questions that you can qualify for discussion if you can come up with at least eight related interpretive follow-up questions for each. When students are struggling to write their own basic questions, I sometimes "give" them a basic question as an intermediate step to writing their own clusters. They then have to develop at least eight of their own related interpretive follow-up questions.

BASIC QUESTION OF INTERPRETATION 2

Why does Gregor's father reject his son so hatefully and violently?

BASIC QUESTION OF INTERPRETATION 3

Does Kafka begin his story with its climax?

BASIC QUESTION OF INTERPRETATION 4

Does Kafka want us to conclude that Gregor's transformation has been for the better or the worse?

ORDINARY PEOPLE
LESSON PLAN 12

Lesson 1: Plot-check quiz on entire novel or sections as assigned. Begin movie version. Make list of 10 important differences (see p. 136).

Lesson 2: Movie version concluded. Discussion of major differences.

Lesson 3: Exercise 1 on film version of the novel. See plot outline.

Lesson 4: Seminar discussions—Exercise 2 (this lesson plan).

Lesson 5: Exercise 3 on the grieving process (Kubler-Ross).

Lesson 6: Exercise 4 on Essay Exam questions.

1. Focus: Review Assignment Sheet: four exercises.

2. Objective: To solve several questions of interpretation about the overall meaning of the novel.

3. Purpose: To increase our mutual understanding (comprehension) and, as a result, our enjoyment of the story and to develop the habit of independent and critical thinking.

4. Input: Begin with a factual quiz to check that everyone has read the novel (Rule 1: No one may participate who has not read the selection). Two or four basic questions (30 or 60 minutes).

5. Modeling, checking, and guided practice: During discussion the coleaders model the four rules of discussion, check for understanding by asking follow-up questions for clarification, substantiation, consistency, relevance, implication, resolution, and to get more opinion. Guided practice is the discussion.

6. Closure: Oral or written resolution of one or two basic questions just discussed.

Note: During Socratic Seminar day(s), in a full 90-minute period, four pairs of student coleaders each lead a 15-minute discussion of the reading. It is important that the teacher approves the student coleader questions before discussion to avoid wasting time on questions that are not clear, factual, or evaluative. (Discussion should center on solving problems, not in trying to figure out what the problems are.) During the remaining time (if any) the teacher leads a demonstration discussion (modeling) of one of his or her basic questions on the reading of the lesson.

Reading: Guest, Judith (1982). *Ordinary People.* New York, Penguin Books.

ORDINARY PEOPLE:
FILM VERSION—SCENE-BY-SCENE PLOT OUTLINE

1. Lake Forest High School choir (Conrad, tenor).

2. Conrad awakes for first day of a new school year.

3. Calvin Jarrett (Donald Sutherland): 41, tax-attorney, Conrad's father. Beth Jarrett (Mary Tyler Moore): 40?, perfectionist, Conrad's mother.

4. Conrad OK? Did he see Doctor Berger?

5. Conrad at breakfast: "You must eat."

6. Lazenby (Conrad's best friend) takes him to school. Train crossing. Cemetery.

7. English class discussion (BQ): "What is your theory on Jim Fawley?" "Was he powerless in the grip of circumstances?" (*Jude the Obscure*)?

8. Conrad calls Dr. Berger for an appointment.

9. Conrad goes to swim team practice.

10. Supper

11. Flashback: boat accident that led to Jordan's (Buck's) death, his older brother.

12. First session with Dr. Berger: depressed? On stage? Home? How long were you in the mental hospital? (8 months) Why? Attempted suicide. Not interested. No problems? Then why are you here? "To be in control. So people don't worry about me?" Brother died in a boating accident. Talking about it "doesn't change a thing."

13. Calvin goes to see Dr. Berger. Not sure why.

14. Swim team practice.

15. Conrad meets Jeannie—outstanding choir member.

16. Halloween.

17. Beth tells Calvin that she wants to go to London for Christmas. Calvin disagrees. He wants a family Christmas at home.

18. Beth in Conrad's room. He tells her that he's not much of a swimmer any more.

19. Dinner party: Beth warns Calvin not to drink too much. He tells Annie that Conrad is seeing a psych. Beth scolds him for using bad judgment.

20. Second session with Dr. Berger: Conrad asks about dreams. Dr. not interested. How do you *feel* now?! Conrad may quit swim team.

21. Conrad meets Karen (a friend from the mental ward): She reminds him and herself of their doctor's statement: "The only one who can help you is yourself." They agree to have a great Christmas and a great year.

22. Conrad in yard with Beth: "Do you remember Buck wanted you to get a dog and you refused? Arf! Arf!

23. Beth in dining room tells Conrad to clean up his room.

24. Third session with Berger: "What do you expect from your mother?" We just don't connect.

25. Calvin talks with Ray, his business partner, who tells him he worries too much.

26. Flashback: Buck and Conrad argue about a shirt.

27. Flashback: Conrad's attempted suicide at home in bathroom.

28. Swim team practice. Coach asks *why* quitting? This is it. No second chances.

29. Lazenby: *Why* did you quit the team? A mistake! Conrad rejects his best friend.

30. Fourth session with Berger: What did your father say about your quitting the team. Contact: control/ many feelings/ "You're mad as hell."

31. Christmas party, argument: "Give her (Beth) the goddamn camera!" Conrad explodes in great anger that surprises his mother *and* himself.

32. Beth tells her mother that she doesn't know how to deal with her son.

33. Choir: Conrad meets Jeannie again. What music do you like? You're a terrific tenor.

34. Conrad calls Karen. No answer.

35. Christmas tree selected. Conrad again explodes at his parents when he tells them that he quit the swim team.

36. Calvin asks Conrad to apologize to his mother: "I'm sorry. I can't talk to her." She hates me.

37. Fifth session with Berger: My mother cannot forgive me for all the terrible things that I have done. She'll never forgive me for messing up her bathroom when I attempted suicide. Berger: "I've learned something. *Who can't forgive who*?! Your mother loves you as much as she is able. She can't express it. You must forgive *yourself!* Conrad: What did I do? Someone has to be responsible.

38. Calvin jogging. You don't see things. She hates me. Don't you see that?

39. Calvin visits Dr. Berger: Conrad *is* better but I don't believe in psych as a panacea. You still feel responsible. It is entirely due to luck that I stopped. Conrad in the middle of his suicide. Both are drifting away from me and I don't know what to do. We've been married 21 years. Beth favored Buck.

40. Calvin: We talked about Buck's funeral and got into a discussion of what color socks I was to wear. How could that *matter*?! Beth hugs him.

41. Shopping mall: Christmas gift list. We should all see Dr. Berger together. Beth replies vehemently that she doesn't need to see a psych! She argues that she and Calvin need time together, to get away. Conrad can stay with mother.

42. Bowling: Jeannie and Conrad. Discussion: She asks if people are punished for what they do? Conrad says no. He's an atheist. Why did you try suicide? Jeannie says she'll see him in choir.

43. Houston: Cal and Beth play golf.

44. Swimming meet: after the contest, Calvin watches his former teammates exit. He punches out one of them who complained about his brother Buck.

45. Calvin calls Karen and finds out that she has killed herself.

46. *Flashback:* the boat accident. Conrad calls Dr. Berger because "I can't get off the hook. It's gotta be somebody's fault. I *didn't* save him. He let go." When are you going to stop blaming yourself? What started this? Karen killed herself. What did you do wrong? I hung on! Jordan's death was not fair. I'm your friend

47. Jeannie and Conrad: Let's try again. Breakfast in her home.

48. Calvin and Beth argue violently over the way they have been treating Conrad.

49. Out of the blue, Conrad hugs his mother. She is dumbfounded.

50. Beth looks for Calvin who is not in bed. She finds him in the dining room. He tells her that she is not strong and asks if she *really* loves him. He continues: "I don't know who you are. I don't know if I love you anymore. How will I cope?"

51. Beth leaves the room without reply. She begins packing, trembling, and crying. She moves out.

52. Conrad: "Dad! What happened?" "You're mother's going away for awhile. Do *not* blame yourself." "Dad, I love you." "I love you too, son."

Note: In the novel, Beth leaves Calvin but in the film he leaves her!

ORDINARY PEOPLE: ASSIGNMENT SHEET

EXERCISE 1: FILM VERSION

A. Are there any significant plot changes that Judith Guest would have rejected? For example, why does Calvin leave Beth in the film while Beth leaves Calvin in the novel? (Ch. 31). See also "Scene-by-Scene Plot Outline." (See p. 136.)

B. Read several student reviews of the novel on Amazon.com. Select one with which you particularly disagree and write a personal letter of rebuttal (one page). Select one with which you entirely agree and explain why you agree in your own movie review for Amazon.com.

C. See Chapter 5 for additional guidelines on conducting a comparison-contrast discussion and follow-up essay on the film version of the original story.

EXERCISE 2: SEMINAR DISCUSSIONS

The novel raises several basic questions of interpretation. Write at least eight specific follow-up questions for one basic question of interpretation (1 or 2) and give a page reference for each. For example: Why is Lazenby the only one who wrote Conrad during his hospital confinement? (p. 96) Or: At the end of the novel when Conrad is finally reconciled with his father, why does he make no mention of his brother? (p. 259)

1. Has Conrad finally learned to cope with the death of Jordan (Buck)?

2. How has Conrad finally learned to cope with the death of his brother?

EXERCISE 3: THE GRIEVING PROCESS

Review Kubler-Ross's description of the stages of the grieving process: denial, anger, bargaining, resignation, and acceptance. Note: these five stages are not linear and they can and do overlap. Indeed, at times a person may get stuck at one stage and skip or never experience a stage at all.

A. Define and illustrate each stage from common experience. (The topic of your example need not be about the death of a loved one but about any major crisis. For example, the news that you are going to have to have a leg amputated or that you will be paralyzed for life.)

B. How does each stage of the grieving process apply or not apply to Conrad, to Calvin, and to Beth? For each character cite an apt passage from the novel (include page reference) that illustrates the state that you believe that character evidences at that moment. What stages are omitted?

Exercise 4: Essay Questions

In a well organized reply to one of these questions, be sure to include specific supporting evidence from the novel. Begin with a thesis statement; omit an introduction.

A. What is the relevance of the poem by Edna St. Vincent Millay (fore piece) to the theme of the novel?

B. Conrad says he is an atheist (p. 251) while his father, Calvin, asks: "How does Christian deal with grief?" (p. 51) Does Christian faith (belief in God's provident love for each of us) help Calvin in his struggle to cope with his son's death?

C. What (or how) does each major character contribute to Conrad's healing? (Beth, Calvin, Karen (Ch. 7 and p. 210 ff), Jeannie (Ch. 30, and p. 100 ff), Dr. Berger, and Lazenby).

ORDINARY PEOPLE:
BASIC QUESTIONS

BASIC QUESTION OF INTERPRETATION 1

Does the author want her readers to conclude that Conrad has finally learned how to cope with the death of his brother?

If *yes*, then:

1. Why did Conrad attempt to kill himself? (pp. 41, 44, 70, 119, 213)

2. At what point does Conrad decide that life is worth living?

3. Did Jordan want life to go on *as if* his brother had not died? (pp. 43, 94, 127)

4. Does the author want us to agree with Karen's approval of Dr. Crawford's statement that "the only one who can help you is you"? (p. 55)

5. In what sense is the Jarrett family "ordinary people"? (pp. 94, 161, 216)

6. Why does Dr. Berger place so much importance on Conrad's feelings? (pp. 98, 136, 225, 251)

7. Who is "the guy in the closet" that Dr. Berger wants Conrad to release? (pp.100, 138)

8. Did Conrad ever release "the guy in the closet"? (pp. 100, 138)

9. At the end of the story when Conrad is finally reconciled with his father, why does he make no mention of his brother? (p. 259)

If *no*, then:

1. Why does Edna St. Vincent Millay speak of man as "a shining animal"? (Fore piece)

2. Who or what did Conrad hold responsible for the death of his brother, Jordan? (p. 120) (Why does Dr. Berger ask, "Who is it who can't forgive who"?)

3. Why did Karen's suicide have such a devastating effect on Conrad? (pp. 210–214)

4. Did Conrad believe for a time that Jordan let go of the overturned boat on purpose? (pp. 218, 224)

5. Why did Conrad believe that it had to be somebody's fault that Jordan died? (p. 224)

6. At the end of the story why does Conrad try to console his father that Beth will eventually return? (pp. 259, 263)

7. Why does the story end with Conrad telling his father that he loves him? (p. 259)

8. Why does Conrad want to play golf with Lazenby? (Epilogue) (p. 262)

9. What is Conrad thanking Dr. Berger for at the end of the story? (p. 260)

10. Why does Dr. Berger regard Conrad as his "prize pupil"? (p. 260)

ALTERNATIVE BASIC QUESTIONS

Here are three more basic questions that you can qualify for discussion if you can come up with at least eight related interpretive follow-up questions for each. When students are struggling to write their own basic questions, I sometimes "give" them a basic question as an intermediate step to writing their own clusters. They then have to develop at least eight of their own related interpretive follow-up questions.

BASIC QUESTION OF INTERPRETATION 2

Who or what was most instrumental in Conrad's learning how to cope with his brother's death?

1. Why is Lazenby the only one who visits Conrad in the hospital after his attempted suicide? (p. 96)

2. When Dr. Burger says Beth loves Conrad "as much as she is able," does he mean that Conrad is wrong to fault her for not helping him to cope with Jordan's death? (p. 120)

3. Why does the author want us to know that Conrad regards himself as an atheist? (p. 251)

4. Does Beth leave Calvin primarily because she disagrees with the way that her husband treats Conrad after his attempted suicide? (p. 252)

5. Is Beth unable to help Conrad because she herself had not accepted Jordan's death? (p. 204)

6. After Conrad's conversation with Jeannie, why does the narrator say "He is in touch for good, with hope, with himself. . .Berger is right, the body never lies." (p. 251)

7. Why couldn't Dr. Crawford help Conrad during his eight months in the hospital? (pp. 41,43, 55)

8. Why does Calvin refer to his son as "this mysterious stranger"? (p. 61)

9. Why does the story end with Conrad telling his father that he loves him? (p. 259)

10. What does Calvin mean when he says that "Grief is ugly. It is isolating"? (p. 127)

11. Why does Dr. Berger place so much importance on Conrad's feelings? (pp. 98, 136, 225, 251)

12. Does Calvin conclude that Jordan's death is also nobody's fault but just "the way things are"? (p. 258)

13. Unlike Dr. Crawford at the hospital who had Conrad speak of Jordan's death "every day," why does Dr. Berger speak so little about it? (pp. 77, 97, 117, 135, 221)

BASIC QUESTION OF INTERPRETATION 3

Why does the author have Calvin ask the question, "How does a Christian deal with grief?" (p. 51)

1. What does Calvin mean when he says "there is no dealing" with grief? (p. 51)

2. What does Calvin mean when he says "the old definitions, the neat, knowing pigeonholes have disappeared or no longer apply" after his son's death? (p. 51)

3. What "unanswered questions" does the reminder of Jordan's death raise in Calvin's mind? (p. 51)

4. What does Calvin mean when he says that "Grief is ugly. It is isolating"? (p. 127)

5. When Calvin visits Dr. Berger, why does he tell him that all of life's events are "accidents"? (p. 146)

6. Why doesn't Calvin speak of Christian faith any where else in the story?

7. Why does Calvin tell Dr. Berger that he doesn't "believe in" psychiatry? (p. 145)

8. Why does Calvin insist that "Life is *not* a series of pathetic, meaningless actions"? (p. 163)

9. Regarding Beth's leaving him, why does Calvin insist that it's nobody's fault, "it is the way things are"? (p. 258)

10. Does Calvin conclude that Jordan's death is also nobody's fault but just "the way things are"? (p. 258)

THE STONE BOY
LESSON PLAN 13

Lesson 1:	Plot-check quiz and discussion of a basic question.
Lesson 2:	The movie version of "The Stone Boy" (90 minutes).
Lesson 3:	Background on the movie with Gina Berriault and discussion of Gene Siskel's movie review (H).
Lesson 4:	Persuasive essay on movie versus short story (H).

1. Focus: Journal writing: Have you ever been disappointed with a film version of a novel or short story that you liked.

2. Objective: To resolve a basic question of interpretation on the short story.

3. Purpose: To increase our mutual understanding and enjoyment of the original story.

4. Input: Begin with a factual plot quiz (H) to check that everyone has read the story. A basic question of interpretation (H).

5. Modeling, checking, and guided practice: During discussion the coleaders model the four rules of discussion, *check for understanding* by asking follow-up questions for clarification, substantiation, consistency, relevance, implication, resolution, and to get more opinion. *Guided practice* IS the discussion.

6. Closure: Oral or written resolution (in the journal) of the basic question just discussed.

Reading: Berriault, Gina (1972). "The Stone Boy" in *Getting Into Books*. Chicago, IL, Great Books Foundation.

THE STONE BOY:
LESSON 1—PLOT-CHECK QUIZ

Directions: On your own paper, next to each number, write a short answer to complete this plot summary of the story. Please do not mark on this quiz.

As the story begins, the Curwing brothers, Arnold and Eugene set out in early morning to (1). Arnold, who is (2) years old, idolizes his older brother who is (3) years old. Arnold wonders if when he reached Eugene's age he would still be (4). As the boys leave the farmhouse, he (5) brings along his (6) in hopes that he might (7). But before they can get to work, a terrible accident (8) occurs. Strangely, after the accident, Arnold does not (9) but rather (10).

When Arnold returns to the farmhouse, he says only that (11). At first, his parents think he is (12). Soon, however, they discover the awful truth that (13). Because of Arnold's behavior (14), many problems arise for him. For example, he (15); as a result, he becomes the film's title character.

Arnold's father and (16) who favors Eugene because (17), take Arnold to Corinth to be questioned by the sheriff. After the sheriff asks if Arnold had been friends with Eugene or if he had been (18) with him, he then asks the all-important question about (19). In reply, Arnold says only that (20). The sheriff then comments that Arnold is "either a (21) or he's so (22) that he's way ahead of us."

After Arnold returns to the farmhouse, visitors arrive who begin to (23) for his behavior after Eugene's death. That night Arnold wants to speak with his mother but she turns him away because she is too (24) to hear his confession of grief. In the morning after she realizes what she has done to hurt her son, she asks Arnold what he wanted the night before. He replies flatly, "I didn't want (25)." Then he walks out the door and down the back steps. He legs tremble from the (26) his answer gave him.

THE STONE BOY:
PLOT-CHECK QUIZ—ANSWER KEY

1. to pick peas
2. 10
3. 17
4. small
5. Arnold
6. rifle (22)
7. bag a duck
8. Eugene is fatally shot
9. get help
10. delays in the field picking peas
11. "Eugene is dead."
12. joking
13. Eugene *is* dead
14. delay in the field
15. is ridiculed for being unfeeling
16. Uncle Andy
17. he looked like him
18. angry
19. why Arnold had delayed in the field
20. he was picking peas
21. moron
22. reasonable
23. shame and ridicule
24. distraught
25. nothing
26. fright

THE STONE BOY:
BASIC QUESTION OF INTERPRETATION

Why do none of the adults in the story understand what Arnold has gone through in killing his brother?

1. Why is Uncle Andy surprised that the sheriff lets Arnold return home after questioning him? (p. 25)

2. What does the sheriff mean when he says in Arnold's presence, "he's either a moron or he's so reasonable that he's way ahead of us"? (p. 25)

3. Why does Arnold's mother refuse to let him come into her bedroom on the night of Eugene's death? (p. 29).

4. Does Arnold's father fail to understand Arnold's grief because his son can offer no reasonable explanation for not running back to the house for help? (p. 31)

5. Why does Berriault reveal to readers the depth of Arnold's grief while none of the adult are able to perceive it? (p. 29)

6. Does Arnold become a stone boy chiefly because none of the adults were able to understand his lack of evident emotion at the loss of his brother?

7. After Uncle Andy's comment during the wake shaming Arnold for his lack of a show of emotion, why does the narrator say, "The men around the room shifted their heavy, satisfying weight of unreasonableness"? (p. 28)

8. When the author ends her story with Arnold's reply to his mother's question that he didn't want anything, is Berriault implying that his parents have lost two sons?

THE STONE BOY:
LESSON 3—AN INTERVIEW WITH GINA BERRIAULT

BACKGROUND ON THE MOVIE

When asked about her inspiration for the film version of "The Stone Boy." Gina Berriault replied, "The idea for the story came from a news item about a hunting accident; and at the time I read it, I was living for the summer on a farm in Montana, and that is where I set the story…But I make up all the persons in the story…It is an original idea."

Was she pleased with her screenplay? "Not really. I was ultimately disappointed in the way that the film turned out." She explained that the screenplay was her attempt to answer the question that students most frequently asked her, "What's going to happen to Arnold?"

1. Given this background information, what do you think it was that made Berriault dissatisfied with her screenplay? [The interviewer did not follow up to ask her to explain her disappointment.]

2. *How* does the movie try to link to two plots—the plot of the original short story (Arnold's rejection by adults) and the plot of the screenplay (the demise of Uncle Andy and Lucille's marriage)?

3. Which, if any, of the connections between the two plots are plausible? For example, why did Arnold go to Reno to apologize to his Aunt Lucille?

Mini-Review: "Silence is not always golden"

Gene Siskel
Chicago Tribune, Thursday, April 26, 1984

Directed by Chris Cain; original screenplay by Gina Berriault; photographed by Juan Ruiz-Anchia; edited by Paul Rubell; music by James Horner; produced by Joe Roth and Ivan Bloch; a 20th Century-Fox release at the Fine Arts Theater. Rated PG.

The Cast

Joe Hillerman	Robert Duvall
Andy Jensen	Frederic Forrest
Ruth Hillerman	Glen Close
George Jensen	Wilford Brimley
Arnold Hillerman	Jason Presson
Lu Jensen	Gail Youngs
Amalie	Cindy Fisher
Nora Hillerman	Susan Blackstone
Eugene Hillerman	Dean Cain

1. If you are excited at the prospect of seeing another Robert Duvall film, you probably will be disappointed with "The Stone Boy." It's not anything that Duvall does; it's what he doesn't do. Even though he receives top billing, his role is one of the smallest in the film. He spends most of his time staring off into the darkness, his back to the camera. Making a similarly limited impression is Glen Close, playing his wife. Indeed, theirs is not the central relationship in this purposefully non-commercial movie.

2. Rather, at the center of "The Stone Boy" is the relationship between a traumatized child and his sensitive, loving grandfather, played by Wilford Brimley, a superb character actor who has his best role in this film. "The Stone Boy" is a drama of silence and communication built upon a tragedy. Set in the big sky country of Montana, "The Stone Boy" opens with two boys, one 12 years old, the other a few years older, leaving their farmhouse to go pick peas.

3. The younger brother has brought along his gun, hoping to bag a wild duck, but before they get to work, a terrible accident occurs. As the boys climb through a fence, the gun gets caught on a wire. Trying to free it, the younger brother accidentally causes the gun to fire, killing his older brother.

4. It's one of those moments that seems both small and monumental. A bullet passes through a body and snuffs out a life. It doesn't seem right that something that small can do so much damage. Those, though are

the thoughts of an adult. No one knows what goes through the mind of 12-year-old Arnold Hillerman [played by Jasson Presson] as he stands in the field, feeling responsible for his brother's death. Instead of running to tell his parents, Arnold stays in the field for some time and in some kind of twisted way to deny what's happened, he begins to pick peas.

5. The delay means nothing, because his brother is dead. But later that delay, that denial, will cause more problems for Arnold, who in silent suffering becomes the film's title character. The rest of "The Stone Boy" follows the forces that keep Arnold in his shell and those that work to free him and his family of their curse of resentment and silence. It's a journey in search of a way to come back from being dead while alive, and the character of the grandfather hold the key. The boys father and mother [Duvall and Close] are too distraught to heal their own son.

6. "The Stone Boy" would be a more commercial film if it narrowed its focus to these four characters: the father, mother, son, and grandfather. But in what may turn out to be a fatal box-office decision, the story has been enlarged to include sizable roles for Close's philandering brother [Frederic Forrest] and his put-upon wife. These two characters rail at each other throughout the movie to no great purpose.

7. The Academy Award-winning Duvall has already received ample praise for his past achievements. So let us now praise Wilford Brimley. There is a quiet power within Brimley that results from his just being there. He comes across as a person who has lived a lot of years and seen a lot of things and probably knows a things or two about life. That describes every character Brimley has played, and those qualities are desperately needed by his grandson in "The Stone Boy." Someone in this family has to reach out and make a connection to this hurting boy.

8. "The Stone Boy" tells the story at a labored pace, not giving in to easy, cathartic drama. That makes it less commercial and a bit frustrating at times to sit through. Nevertheless, "The Stone Boy" reveals in detail the works that goes into the art of healing and that is a subject foreign to most American movies. For that reason, "The Stone Boy" is recommended.

THE STONE BOY:
MOVIE REVIEW

Directions: As you read Siskel's movie review make notations on your copy and then answer these questions in complete sentences in your journal.

Before viewing the movie version

1. Why does Siskel think we will be disappointed with the movie version of Gina Berriault's story?

2. Why does Siskel think that Arnold picked peas after his brother's death?

3. Based on your reading of the original story, do you agree with Siskel's interpretation of Arnold's behavior after Eugene's death? If so, why so? If not, why not?

4. In the original story, why does no one reach out to help Arnold cope with the loss of his brother?

5. What is Siskel's chief objection to the movie?

6. In spite of his objections, why does Siskel still recommend the movie?

7. Explain how, specifically, Siskel's movie review is a model of good writing.

After viewing the movie version

8. Unlike the short story, why does the movie concentrate not on Arnold's growing isolation but on the sympathetic relationship between Arnold and his loving grandfather?

9. Do you agree with Siskel that "the philandering brother" [uncle Andy] of Arnold's mother [Ruth] and his "put-upon wife" [Lucille] rail at each other for no dramatic purpose? If so, why so? If not, why not?

10. Unlike the movie, does the short story imply that the Curwing have lost two sons? If so, why? If not, why not?

11. List three specific changes that you liked in the movie.

12. List three specific changes that you disliked in the movie.

THE STONE BOY:
PERSUASIVE ESSAY—THINK SHEET

Purpose: To convince your reader to agree with your thesis by stating clearly and explaining at least three supporting reasons for your agreement or disagreement with Berriault's or Siskel's opinion of the movie. You must also include a counter argument and rebuttal for each of your three arguments.

Tentative thesis:

Organization:

Arguments [reasons]	Evidence [examples, explanations]
1. First	1.
Objection	Rebuttal
2. More important	2.
Objection	Rebuttal
3. Most important	3.
Objection	Rebuttal

English _____   Name_____

THE STONE BOY:
PERSUASIVE ESSAY—GRADE SHEET

The grade assigned is my judgment of the quality of the essay as a whole. I reward writers for what they do well and I do not ordinarily mark individual errors. Because this grade sheet describes the criteria for each grade level, you will know why your essay is a B rather than an A and so on. If you disagree with the grade assigned, see me for a writing conference. If you wish, you may then revise your paper to improve your final grade. *Note:* Assemble your papers in this order: (1) grade sheet (on top), (2) final copy, (3) checklist, (4) first copy, and (5) think sheet

(A+ 200) (A 190) (A-180)

The introduction hooks the reader's attention and leads into a clearly stated thesis that agrees or disagrees with Siskel's review *or* makes a value judgment about Berriault's movie version. The development of the essay illustrates with specific examples (from the movie, the original short story, or the movie review) the thesis and includes three counter arguments and a rebuttal of each. The essay is clearly organized and ends with a sense of finality. These papers demonstrate stylistic maturity in diction, syntax, and knowledge of the MLA format. The writing need not be flawless but reveals the writer's grasp and use of Standard English.

(B+ 175) (B 165) (B- 160)

These essays present a clearly stated thesis but do not adequately illustrate, with specific examples, the reasons for the position taken As a result, these papers are not as convincing as the top papers because they lack development. Some lapses in diction or syntax may be present, but the writing is organized well enough to present the writer's ideas clearly. Nevertheless, these papers lack the persuasive force of papers in the A range.

(C+ 155) (C 145) (C- 140)

These essays address the purpose of the assignment to persuade the reader to agree with Berriault that the movie is a near failure or that Siskel's review is right or wrong. However, these papers lack development and are not as clearly organized as papers in the B range. As a result, their arguments are not as convincing. They also reveal inconsistent control of sentence structure (variety of lengths and openings), lapses in diction, use of Standard English and the MLA format.

(D+ 135) (D 130) (D- 120)

D papers have one or more major errors: the thesis is not clearly stated; lack of development (examples explained sufficiently), weak counter arguments and rebuttals or none at all, weak organization; weak control of diction, syntax, and/or usage.

INC *(no grade):* These papers do not address the purpose of the assignment. A writing conference is mandatory for a passing grade.

HARRISON BERGERON
LESSON PLAN 14

1. Focus: Journal writing: Is the desire to be the best as strong in human nature as the desire to be average or ordinary? (10 minutes)

2. Objective: To resolve a basic question of interpretation about the overall meaning of the story.

3. Purpose: To increase our mutual understanding (comprehension) and, as a result, our enjoyment of the story. To develop the habit of independent and critical thinking.

4. Input: Begin with a factual quiz (handout follows) to check that everyone has read the story (Rule 1: No one may participate who has not read the selection). The quiz should be 10 factual questions, short answers (not true/false). Those with 70% are in the inner circle; those with less are in the outer circle (15 minutes). Basic question. Handout follows (30–40 minutes).

5. Modeling, checking, and guided practice: During discussion the coleaders *model* the four rules of discussion, *check for understanding* by asking follow-up questions for clarification, substantiation, consistency, relevance, implication, resolution, and to get more opinion. *Guided practice* IS the discussion.

6. Closure: Oral or written resolution of one or two basic questions just discussed.

Note: During Socratic Seminar day(s), in a full 90-minute period, four pairs of student coleaders each lead a 15-minute discussion of the reading. It is important that the teacher approves the student coleader questions before discussion to avoid wasting time on questions that are not clear, are factual, or evaluative. (Discussion should center on solving problems, not in trying to figure out what the problems are.) During the remaining time (if any) the teacher leads a demonstration discussion (modeling) of one of his or her basic questions on the reading of the lesson.

Reading: Vonnegut, K. (1981)."Harrison Bergeron." *Short Stories: Characters in Conflict.* Warriner, J. Ed. New York: Harcourt Brace Jananovich.

HARRISON BERGERON:
PLOT-CHECK QUIZ

Directions: Answer each question in the space beneath it in a brief sentence or two. Do not repeat the question in your answer.

1. What two kinds of equality had been achieved in the year 2081?

2. In what two ways had these two kinds of equality been achieved?

3. Why is Harrison such a problem for the authorities of 2081?

4. What kind of handicaps did George have?

5. Why does Harrison's mother, Hazel, have no handicaps?

6. What is George's opinion of the government that handicapped him?

7. How does Harrison revolt against the system of handicaps?

8. Does anyone join Harrison's revolt?

9. Why does Harrison's revolt fail?

10. Do George and Hazel realize what had happened to their son at the story's end?

HARRISON BERGERON:
PLOT-CHECK QUIZ—ANSWER KEY

Directions: Answer each question in the space beneath it in a brief sentence or two. Do not repeat the question in your answer.

1. What two kinds of equality had been achieved in the year 2081?

   People in 2081 were not only equal before God and the law, "they were equal every which way"—everyone was virtually the same.

2. In what two ways had these two kinds of equality been achieved?

   Passage of three Constitutional Amendments (211–213) and the vigilance of the U.S. Handicapper General, Diana Moon Glampers, brought about all this equality.

3. Why is Harrison such a problem for the authorities of 2081?

   At 14, Harrison Bergeron, a genius, an athlete and exactly 7 feet tall, outgrew handicaps faster than the H-G men could think of and apply them.

4. What kind of handicaps did George have?

   George has a little mental handicap radio in his ear to keep him from taking unfair advantage of his brain.

5. Why does Harrison's mother, Hazel, have no handicaps?

   Hazel is already perfectly normal in every way.

6. What is George's opinion of the government that handicapped him?

   George defends the government that handicaps him because it eliminates competition among citizens as long as they observe the law to keep on their handicaps.

7. How does Harrison revolt against the system of handicaps?

   On public television, in a recording studio, Harrison declares himself emperor and orders everyone to do as he says because "he [is] a greater ruler than any man who ever lived." He then overcomes the laws of gravity and motion.

8. Does anyone join Harrison's revolt?

   At his request to be his Empress, a "blindingly beautiful" ballerina arose to join Harrison's defiance of the laws of gravity and motion.

9. Why does Harrison's revolt fail?

   Diana Moon Glampers enters the television studio with a double-barreled 10-gauge shotgun and immediately kills Harrison and the ballerina. After reloading, she orders everyone to put back on their handicaps. Everyone does so.

10. Do George and Hazel realize what had happened to their son at the story's end?

    Not really. Hazel tells George that "something real sad" happened on television while he had gone to the kitchen to get a can of beer. The story ends with George telling his wife to forget sad things.

HARRISON BERGERON:
BASIC QUESTION OF INTERPRETATION

According to Vonnegut's story, is the desire to excel as strong as the tendency to be mediocre? *Rephrased:* According to the story, is the urge to be better than average as strong as the inclination to be ordinary?

If *yes*, then:

1. Why does Hazel consider herself an authority on what is "normal"? (p. 11)

2. Why does George defend the system that handicaps him even though his intelligence is "way above normal"? (p. 12)

3. Why is competition a dirty word in the world of 2081? (p. 12)

4. Why does the playing of the musicians improve only after Harrison physically threatens them? (p. 16)

5. Why does only one person join Harrison's revolt? (p. 15)

6. Why does Vonnegut have Harrison's revolt fail? (p. 17)

7. Does Vonnegut want us to conclude that people like Harrison are as much a danger to society as are people like Hazel and George? (pp. 13, 15)

If *no*, then:

8. Why is the Government of 2081 concerned more with maintaining mediocrity than with encouraging excellence? (p. 10)

9. Why is the "unceasing vigilance" of the Handicapper General's agents needed to maintain equality "every which way"? (p. 10)

10. Why are the penalties for removing a handicap so severe? (p. 12)

11. Why is everyone cautioned not to try to reason with Harrison? (p. 13)

12. Why does the author have a ballerina voluntarily join Harrison's revolt? (p. 15)

13. Why does Vonnegut have Harrison defy not only civil laws but also the laws of gravity and motion? (p. 16)

14. Why does the story end with the Handicapper General back in charge? (p. 17)

5

SOCRATIC SEMINARS ON FILM CRITICISM

Few teachers would deny that one powerful way to make literature come alive to convey its dramatic power is to have students view the movie version of a novel, play, or short story whenever possible. However, some teachers do not seem to realize that when they show a film, the film should *become* the teacher. In other words, showing a film without making it an *active* learning experience reduces it to mere entertainment. It becomes "mere entertainment" when students are allowed to be passive spectators who have not been invited and challenged to reflect on what they are viewing.

Lesson plans 15–20 center on comparison-contrast discussions and follow-up comparison-contrast and persuasive essays (for assessments). In each case, be it a novel, short story, or a Shakespearean play, students become aware that when a movie director changes the plot of a story in any significant way, he necessarily alters the theme—the overall meaning of the plot. Such changes *should* make students wonder if the author of the original story would have approved. If so, why? If not, why not?

Two useful textbooks for writing about and discussing films based on novels, plays, or short stories are by William Costanzo, *Teaching the Movies: Twelve Great Films on Video and How to Teach Them* (1992) and Jan Bone and Ron Johnson, *Understanding the Film: An Introduction to Film Appreciation*, 5th edition (1997).

GUIDELINES FOR WRITING ABOUT MOVIES BASED ON NOVELS OR SHORT STORIES

FOUR PREWRITING EXERCISES

- Exercise 1: Make notations on what has been *added, omitted, and retained* from the original story.

- Exercise 2: Make notations on *what is important*, what you *do not understand*, what you particularly *liked* (something that moved you emotionally) and/or *disliked*, and on what is related (one part of the story to another, notice connections).

- Exercise 3: List *10 important differences* between the movie and the short story or the novel.

- Exercise 4: List *10 important similarities* between the movie and the short story or the novel.

GUIDELINES FOR EXERCISES 3 AND 4

Note: You have the option of doing these two exercises with a partner. Put both names on the paper; you will receive the same grade. Unless you follow these guidelines exactly, your paper will be returned (INC) without a grade.

1. Each difference or similarity between the movie and the text (short story or novel) must be written as *a complete sentence.*

2. In each sentence, *refer to both the movie and the story.*

3. *No two sentences may begin the same way;* the sentence openings must be varied.

4. *Number* each difference or similarity and *skip a line* between each sentence.

5. *Circle* the numbers of what you regard as the *three most important* differences or similarities. Rank in order of importance.

6. As always, use ink (no pencil, ever), write on standard paper (not spiral, ever), and put the proper heading on the upper right-hand corner.

7. Avoid wordiness; try to be as concise as possible. Use active voice whenever possible.

GLUE WORDS FOR DIFFERENCES

but, however, unlike, in contrast, although, as if, on the other hand, still, nevertheless, yet, rather than, despite, in spite of, instead of, contrary to

GLUE WORDS FOR SIMILARITIES

similarly, in like anner, just as, in the same way, like, as, equally, similar to

GLUE WORDS FOR RANKING

first, second, finally, more important, most important, another, furthermore, mreover, in addition, again, of primary importance, the least, the greatest

MODELS

The example that follows uses *Barn Burning,* which is the subject of Lesson Plan 15.

1. In the movie, Sarty accidentally learns the truth about his father's sordid past but in the short story he remains uninformed.

2. Similar to the opening of the short story, in the movie Sarty is expected to lie at his father's trial.

3. Most important, unlike the short story, in the movie Sarty looks back.

THE MOVIE REVIEW

Assignment: Write a 250-word (one page, double-spaced, typed) movie review of a film. Include a topic outline, as well as the first and final copy (staple on top).

Purpose: To convince your reader that he or she should or should not see the film.

Prewriting: Read two model reviews. *Discussion:* why do people read movie reviews? What are they looking for? What do they expect to find? Given these two models, what is an important characteristic of a good review? Why do movie critics avoid giving too much plot summary?

GENERIC OUTLINE

1. *Introduction:* hook the attention of your reader with a startling fact, statistic, or intriguing statement.

2. Your *thesis* (pro or con) should be clearly stated as part of the introduction. (First paragraph: 1 and 2.)

3. Second paragraph: give a *brief plot summary,* that is, enough to let your reader know what the movie is about but not so much that you lay out the entire story.

4. Third paragraph: state *and* explain at least *two reasons* for your pro or con position.

5. *Conclude* with your final recommendation by rephrasing your thesis.

BARN BURNING
LESSON PLAN 15

Lesson 1   Reading and discussion of a basic question of *Barn Burning*. Plot-check quiz (handout) and discussion of a basic question.

Lesson 2   Make notations while viewing the film version of the story. Follow the film guidelines.

Lesson 3   Discussion of major film differences and why Faulkner would have rejected the film's resolution of his story.

1. Focus: Why would Faulkner, himself a former Hollywood screen writer, have rejected this film version of his story?

2. Objective: To participate in a comparison-contrast discussion of the film version of the story and to write a follow-up comparison-contrast essay.

3. Purpose: To realize that a film version of a story is the interpretation of director Peter Werner and screenwriter Horton Foote.

4. Input: Before viewing the film: Plot-check quiz of the short story followed by discussion of a Basic Question of Interpretation 1: "Why does Faulkner want us to admire Sarty's decision to turn against his father's barn burnings?" Film version of the story: "Barn Burning," The American Short Story Collection. Monterey Home Video, 1980, 40 minutes. Starring Tommy Lee Jones as Abner and Shawn Whittington as Sarty Snopes.

5. Modeling: After viewing the film: Model some examples on an overhead of how to write a few differences between the film and the story.

6. Checking for   Review guidelines for writing differences between the film and
    understanding: the original story.

7. Guided practice: After viewing the film: Discussion of the significance of major differences between the film and the story followed by discussion of a Basic Question of Interpretation 2: "Why would Faulkner have rejected this film version of his story even though it also has Sarty reject his father's barn burnings?"

8. Closure: Comparison-contrast follow-up essay and/or a movie review of the film. Follow the Film Guidelines.

Reading: William Faulkner, "Barn Burning" in *The American Short Story*, Vol. 2. Skaggs, Calvin, Ed. New York, Dell Publishers, 1980, pp. 374–392.

Internet: "William Faulkner's Short Stories" http://www.mcsr.olemiss.edu/egjbp/faulkner/stories.html

BARN BURNING:
FILM VS. FAULKNER—BASIC QUESTIONS
BASIC QUESTION OF INTERPRETATION 1

Why does Faulkner want us to admire Sarty's decision to turn against his father's barn burnings?

1. Why is Sarty the only member of the Snopes family to turn against Abner?

2. Is Sarty intimidated by his father or is he ashamed of his barn burnings? (pp. 378, 389)

3. Why does the narrator tells us that 20 years later Sarty understood that his father confused truth and justice with spite and revenge? (p. 378)

4. When Sarty first sees Major de Spain's courthouse-size home, why does he think that "these people" would be "impervious to the puny flames" that his father might contrive? (p. 380)

5. Why does Sarty keep defending his father and hope that he will reform when there seems to be no evidence upon which to base his hope?

6. At what point in the story does Sarty reject his father's rationalization for his barn burnings that he must stick to his own blood?

7. When his father orders Sarty to get the coal-oil can to burn Major de Spain's barn, why does he consider running away but then say that he can't do it? (p. 389)

8. Even after Major de Spain's barn has been destroyed, why does Sarty insist that his father was brave? (p. 392)

9. At the end of the story, why does the author want us to know that Sarty is misinformed about his father's sordid past as a thief, deserter, and a mercenary? (pp. 376, 392)

10. Why does Faulkner end his story with the laconic sentence, "He did not look back"? (p. 392)

BASIC QUESTION OF INTERPRETATION 2

Why would Faulkner not have approved the movie version of his story even though it also has Sarty reject his father's barn burnings?

1. Why is Sarty the only one in the family to defy Abner?

2. Does Sarty look as though he is ten years old in both the movie and the story?

3. In the movie but not the story, why does Abner give Sarty a lecture about a man knowing when and how to take his own justice?

4. Why does the movie add the scene when Sarty is cleaning a rabbit?

5. During lunch, why does Abner give Sarty a pocket knife in the movie but not in the story?

6. Unlike the story, why does Sarty find out in the movie that his father had been a traitor, a thief, and a mercenary during the Civil War?

7. More in the movie than in the story, why does Sarty hope against hope that his father will reform?

8. Why does Sarty defend his father more in the movie than in the story?

9. Why does Sarty refuse to get the oil can in the movie but not in the story?

10. Does Sarty finally decide to go against his father at a moment different in the story than he does in the movie?

11. Why does the movie have Lennie and Abner survive while in the original story they are killed by Major de Spain?

12. Why does the story end with Sarty still defending his father while the movie ends with Sarty standing in a field in the morning watching his family leave?

13. Unlike the movie, why does the story end with the laconic sentence, "He did not look back"?

BARN BURNING:
PLOT-CHECK QUIZ

Directions: Please do not mark on this quiz. Put your answers on a separate sheet of paper to hand in. The answers below may be used once, more than once, or not at all since some of them are false. The statements are in chronological order.

Colonel Sartoris	Net Snopes	Harris	Abner
Colonel Sartoris Snopes	Sarty's sisters	Miss Lula	Lennie Snopes
Major de Spain	Lizzie	Wilson	fire
steel	water	Enemy	gun powder
1870	1880	1890+	1865

The story opens with him (1) accusing him (2) of burning his barn. At the trial, he (3) believes that he must lie to defend him (4) from them (5). But he (6) is found not guilty because of (7). He (8) had been wounded in the Civil War which had taken place (9) years earlier than the present time of the story. Hence, the story takes place in (10). The father of the narrator of the story (11) had been wounded during the Civil War by (12). The father's sense of independence was so "wolf-like" that he refused to (13). "Big, hulking, lethargic, and bovine" are Faulkner's adjectives to describe them (14).

"The element of (15) spoke of some deep main-spring of his (16) being, as the element of steel or powder spoke to other men, as the one weapon for the preservation of [his] integrity."

He (17) goes to have a word with the man (18) who he felt would "own" him body and soul for the next eight months. When he (19) purposely ruined his (20) expensive rug, she (21) became very upset and demanded that he leave her home. After returning to his own home, she (22) wanted to clean the soiled rug but he (23) insisted on doing the job himself. As a result, the rug was entirely (24) because he had put a (25) in it.

Once again, he (26) was back in court but this time "the incredible circumstance" was that he (27) was being sued by one of his own tenants. He (28) claimed that (29) bushels of corn was too high a price to pay for the damage to his (30) rug. To be more than fair, the magistrate reduced the fine to (31) bushels of corn. However, when it became clear that he (32) now intended to (33), he (34) made his momentous and irrevocable decision to (35).

But this barn burning ended in tragedy: (36) and (37) were killed and he (38) went off into the woods. Ironically, this person (39) still mistakenly thought that he (40) had truly fought in his (41) cavalry. Faulkner ends his story dramatically and laconically with the shortest (five-word) sentence (42) of the story.

Score: 42 × 2 = 84 + 1 = 85 points possible

BARN BURNING:
PLOT QUIZ—ANSWER KEY

1. Harris
2. Abner Snopes
3. Sarty Snopes; (Colonel Sartoris Snopes)
4. His father, Abner
5. the Enemy
6. Abner
7. Lack of evidence
8. Abner
9. Thirty
10. 1890+
11. Sarty
12. musket ball in his leg
13. cooperate with any man
14. Sarty's sisters
15. fire
16. Abner's
17. Abner
18. Major de Spain
19. Abner
20. Major de Spain's
21. Miss Lula

22. Sarty's mother, Mrs. Snopes
23. Abner
24. ruined
25. hole
26. Abner
27. Major de Spain
28. Abner
29. twenty
30. Major de Spain's
31. ten
32. Abner
33. burn de Spain's barn
34. Sarty
35. leave home, betray Abner, warn Major de Spain
36. Abner (Lennie)
37. Lennie (Abner)
38. Sarty
39. Sarty
40. Abner
41. Colonel Sartoris
42. "He did not look back."

BARN BURNING:
COMPARISON/CONTRAST ESSAY—THINK SHEET

Purpose: To explain how three key plot changes in the movie version of Faulkner's "Barn Burning" distort the theme of the original story.

Thesis: Write your revised and approved thesis statement here (first paragraph).

Development:
First difference (topic sentence, second paragraph, least important change):

Second difference (topic sentence, third paragraph, a more important change):

Third difference (topic sentence, fourth paragraph, the most important change):

Concluding sentence (fifth paragraph):

Barn Burning:
Comparison/Contrast Essay

The grade assigned your paper reflects my judgment of the quality of the essay *as a whole*. I reward you for what you do well and I do not mark individual errors. This grade sheet explains the criteria for each grade level so that you will be able to understand why your paper is a B rather than an A or a C rather than a B and so on. If you disagree with the grade given your paper, see me for a writing conference and I will explain in more detail the reasons for giving the grade that I did to your paper. You may revise your essay if you see me for a writing conference during lunch.

A [200, 190, 180]

The introduction arouses reader interest and leads into a clearly stated thesis about specific differences that improve or weaken the original story. The essay is well developed because it explains sufficiently the implications of at least three major differences and concludes with a sense of finality. These papers demonstrate stylistic maturity since they are clearly written and organized and employ appropriate diction. The writing need not be without flaws but reveals the writer's overall competence.

B [175, 168, 160]

These papers present a clearly stated thesis about differences that improve or distort Faulkner's story but do not adequately explain the implications of those differences. As a result, these essays lack development of basic insights. They are written in an appropriate style but with less maturity than the top papers. Some lapses in diction and syntax may appear, but the writing demonstrates sufficient control of the elements of composition to present the writer's idea's clearly.

C [155, 148, 140]

These essays address the purpose of the assignment to contrast the movie with the short story but they do not demonstrate an adequate understanding of the implications of the differences between the two. Sometimes the writer fails to discriminate between major and minor changes. These papers are written adequately but demonstrate inconsistent control of sentence structure, diction, and the use of Standard English.

D [135, 128, 120]

These papers have one or more of these major flaws: a failure to state a thesis that is a value judgment about the differences between the move and the story; a failure to explain the connection between the differences and the thesis; a failure to identify major differences; an assertion of general statements without supporting textual evidence. The writing conveys the writer's ideas but reveals flaws in diction, syntax, or organization. These essays may contain consistent spelling errors and flaws in grammar.

F [NO GRADE]

These essays fail to address the purpose of the assignment and must be revised after a writing conference to receive a passing grade.

BARN BURNING:
VOCABULARY QUIZ

Directions: The words below may be used only once to complete the meaning of a sentence. After choosing a word, write it on your answer sheet and put its part of speech on the same line in parenthesis (N, V, ADJ, or ADV). This is the odd number. On the line beneath the word chosen, give its definition or synonym. This is the even number.

exultant	irascible	implacable	burlesque	vile
bovine	integrity	lethargic	mercenary	impervious
burlesque	incredulous	discretion	voracious	exultant

Sarty never did learn the truth about his father's (1–2) past—that he was a horse thief as well as a (3–4) during the Civil War. In short, Abner had no (5–6).

Faulkner described Sarty's twin sisters as (7–8) because they were so (9–10) and displayed no interest in work.

Sarty mistakenly thought that Major de Spain would be (11–12) to his father's (13–14) hatred for those who he thought owned him "body and soul."

Only the word (15–16) describes Abner's chutzpah in taking Major de Spain to court for demanding compensation for the rug that Abner had ruined.

Because he lacked (17–18), Lennie neither questioned nor challenged his father's barn burnings.

Unlike the O. J. Simpson trial where the evidence was overwhelming, Abner's first trial was still a (19–20) of justice because of lack of evidence.

The mix of Abner's (21–22) need for revenge, Major de Spain's (23–24) nature were the ingredients for tragedy.

Because he still truly believed that his father was a brave man, indeed a war hero, it was with (25–26) pain that Sarty finally made the moral decision to reject his father's evil ways.

How Sarty was able to (27–28) the difference between good and evil at such a young age remains one of the unanswered questions of Faulkner's story.

The story ends on an (29–30) tone when Faulkner says of his young hero, "He did not look back.

Barn Burning:
Vocabulary Quiz—Answer Key

1. vile (ADJ)

2. evil, wicked

3. mercenary (ADJ)

4. working merely for money

5. integrity (N)

6. personal honesty

7. bovine (ADJ)

8. cow-like, dull, stupid

9. lethargic (ADJ)

10. sluggish, apathetic

11. impervious (ADJ)

12. unaffected by, immune

13. voracious (ADJ)

14. insatiable, greedy

15. incredulous (ADJ)

16. unbelievable

17. discretion (N)

18. judgment, discernment

19. burlesque (ADJ)

20. travesty, tawdry show

21. implacable (ADJ)

22. unstoppable

23. irascible (ADJ)

24. hot-tempered

25. excruciating (ADJ)

26. unbearable, intensely painful

27. divine (V)

28. discover, discern

29. exultant (ADJ)

30. joyful, rejoicing greatly

SCORE: 15 words × 3 = 45 points possible: 1 point each for the correct word, the part of speech, and definition or synonym.

BARN BURNING:
FILM NOTATION SHEET

Faulkner	*Film*

1. Sunday: A trial Abner Snopes *v* Harris (374–76)   1. _____

2. Outside store: Sarty attacks a name-caller, Barn Burner (376–77)   2. _____

3. Family camps overnight in woods: Abner confronts Sarty about blood loyalty (377–79).   3. _____

4. Family moves to de Spain plantation: Abner and Sarty visit his mansion and Abner ruins his rug. White sweat? (379–82).   4. _____

5. Back home: the Major returns the rug demanding that it be cleaned; again, Abner purposely ruins it. (382–83)   5. _____

6. Abner returns the rug to Major de Spain (383–84)   6. _____

7. Back home: the Major confronts Abner demanding retribution (384–85).   7. _____

8. Wednesday: While plowing with Lennie, Sarty still hopes Abner will reform. (385)   8. _____

9. Saturday: A second trial—Snopes v de Spain! (386–87).   9. _____

10. At the blacksmith's shop, Abner and his sons have lunch. (387–88).   10. _____

11. Back home: "Abner! No!" (389)   11. _____

12. Sarty warns Major de Spain, Abner and Lennie are killed (390–92)   12. _____

13. Resolution: "He [Sarty] did not look back."   13. _____

TWO SOLDIERS
LESSON PLAN 16

Three-Day Unit

Film: "Two Soldiers," The American Short Story Collection. Starring Huckleberry Fox; 60 minutes. (AW Peller & Associates, 116 Washington Ave., PO Box 106, Hawthorne, NJ 07507-0106; www.awpeller.com)

Reading: William Faulkner, "Two Soldiers," *Collected Stories of William Faulkner.* New York, Vintage Books, 1995, pp. 81–99.

Internet: "William Faulkner's Short Stories" — http://www.mscr.olemiss.edu/egjbp/faulkner/stories.html

Lesson 1:   Factual quiz on the story. While viewing film version of the story, list 10 important differences between the two.

Lesson 2:   Write your own resolution to the story and then compare yours with five student models (Exercises 1 and 2).

Lesson 3:   Write an essay on why Faulkner would not have approved the film's resolution to his story (Exercise 4).

1.	Focus:	Should movie producers and directors remain faithful to an author's original story? If so, why so? If not, why not?
2.	Objective:	To understand how changing the plot changes the meaning (theme) of a story.
3.	Purpose:	To understand why Faulkner would not have approved of the resolution in the movie version. (It changes his theme.)
4.	Input:	Begin with a plot-check quiz.
5.	Modeling, checking, and guided practice:	While viewing VHR make up a list of 10 important differences between the film and the original story. (40 minutes)
6.	Closure:	See guidelines for writing your own resolution to the story and an essay on why Faulkner would not have approved the movie's resolution.

Note: For the follow-up exercises, you must have deleted the last paragraph, the resolution, of Faulkner's story. Perceptive students will notice that without this paragraph, the story stops but does not end.

TWO SOLDIERS:
FACTUAL QUIZ

Directions: Choose the best answer by marking the scantron form. Please do not write on this test.

1. "Me and Pete," the first three words of the story, refers to:

   a. Billy Joe and brother
   b. The narrator and cousin
   c. The narrator and brother

2. The narrator of the story is almost _____ years old.

   a. 9   b. 10   c. 15   d. 17   e. 20

3. Pete is almost _____ years old. See #2 (a–e).

4. Most of the story takes place in:

   a. Memphis b. Oxford c. Frenchman's d. Mississippi e. Jefferson
                              Bend

5. The time of the story is during the _____ War.

   a. First   b. Second   c. Civil   d. None of these

6. Pete goes to the city to:

   a. enlist in the Army
   b. get a job
   c. go to school
   d. pay a debt
   e. None of these

7. When Pete left home, he was most concerned about the effect his absence would have on his:

   a. Maw   b. Pap   c. brother   d. sister   e. None of these

8. Pete's mother is against his leaving home because:

   a. She can't think of one good reason.
   b. She thinks that her brother had done enough.
   c. She knows he will get into trouble.
   d. She thinks his brother will want to leave home.
   e. None of these.

9. Pete's father is against his leaving home because:

   a. He had done enough already.
   b. He needed Pete's help on the farm.
   c. He had gotten into trouble himself.
   d. He agreed with Pete's mother's thinking.
   e. None of these.

10. Pete's brother is both for and against his brother's leaving home.

   a. True   b. False

11. Since Pete felt that he had to leave home, that he's "got to go," his brother assumed that he would have to go with him.

a. True   b. False

12. Pete never did give a reason for leaving home.

a. True   b. False

13. The author wants us to admire Pete's reason for leaving home.

a. True   b. False

14. The author wants us to think that Pete's brother is foolish for wanting to leave home with his brother.

a. True   b. False

15. Pete's brother finally gets to the city where Pete had gone by:

a. Walking b. Walking and riding c. Hitchhiking d. Bus e. Train

16. When Pete finally gets to Memphis and finds his brother, Pete is:

a. Bewildered b. Astonished c. Disgusted d. Angry e. Embarrassed

17. Pete immediately reprimands his brother for:

a. Using profane language	b. Using his knife	c. Whining and whimpering	d. Disobeying him	e. Not telling his parents he had also left home

18. Peter's brother told him that he had come to Memphis because:

a. He wanted to say good-by	b. His heart hurt	c. He knew he wanted him to come	d. He knew he would need wood and water	e. None of these

19. Pete's brother is astonished when his older brother:

a. Hits him on the head	b. Told him he had embarrassed him	c. Kisses him	d. Screams at him for coming to find him	e. None of these

20. Pete's brother returned home because he knew:

a. He was too young to remain	b. His parents would be worried he had run away	c. His brother told him to do so	d. He needed more money	e. He really could not be of any help

TWO SOLDIERS:
THE RESOLUTION

EXERCISE 1

Write your own resolution to the story. You probably noticed that this story stops but does not end (the last paragraph has been omitted). It has no resolution.

- A. *Begin* by listing any question or questions about the story that seem unanswered. Why do you still want to know about Pete's brother?

- B. *Reread the last page* of the story beginning with the sentence, "She had a car." Be sure to make notations on your copy about the way the boy tells his story.

- C. What is distinctive or unique about the style of the story teller, Pete's little brother? Try to be as specific as possible.

- D. *Write your own resolution to the story.* Try to anticipate how you think Faulkner ends his story. Write a resolution to the story that answers the above question(s) *and* imitates the style and tone of the nine-year old narrator.

EXERCISE 2

Compare the five student resolutions (handout) with the original. Which is closest to Faulkner's in style and tone?

How close did you come to Faulkner's ending? How can you explain the differences? *Explain your answer in a paragraph on a separate sheet.*

EXERCISE 3
(OPTIONAL/EXTRA CREDIT)

Revise in Standard (correct) English (on your own paper) the concluding paragraph of Faulkner's story. Compare your revision with the author's original paragraph. What has happened to the tone of the passage? Why?

EXERCISE 4

How does the movie version of the story end? Why would Faulkner have disapproved of this ending? Begin with a topic sentence that states the difference between the two endings and then *explain in a one-page essay* two or three reasons for Faulkner's rejection of the movie's resolution.

TWO SOLDIERS:
FIVE STUDENT RESOLUTIONS

Discussion: Which one of these five resolutions to the short story best imitates the style and tone of the nine-year-old narrator?

1. We had drove fer 'bout 15 minutes an I fell asleep. I reckon it was 'bout an hour before I was waked up. We was in some town at a eatin place an we et some mighty good ham 'n eggs 'n I had most of what seemed like a pot of coffee. The soldier paid fer the food an didn't stop-a-tall 'till we was home and he waked me up again so's I gitted outa the car an walked up to the door and went in. Maw was settin in her rocker an Pap was still off in the field or sumpin. Maw said, "Well, we figgered you'd come home iffen you got hungry." I said, "I had to go to tell Pete goodby." Then Maw said, "So that's where you were. We figgered you'd done somethin' like that."

2   When I headed fer da car dis other soldier with lots of buttons hopped in fron of me and opened up the door. We was driven through all the town that I came though goin the other way. The soldier was very quiet and he was listen to the radio. But it was not what Pete and me listen to at Old Man Killegrew's. He was listen to some funny music with some lady hollerin in the background. About eighty miles later, my stomach made a loud noise and jest after that the soldier stopped at some nice place to eat. After we ate we left. The car drove up to the mailbox and I got out. When Maw saw me, she came runnin out of the house. She dropped to her knees and gave be a great big bear hug. Then she told me that if I ever did that again she'd beat the livin tar outa me.

3   Me and the driver sat in the car for two and a half hours and said nothing. As we was gettin into Jefferson County, I asked the soldier, "Would you watch o'er my Pete for me?" The soldier said Pete would be just fine. When we got to the mail box, I got out, said 'bye and he was gone. My legs were wobblin as I got to the door. Before I knowed it, there was Maw and Paw to get me a big ole hug. While we was all crying, Maw said, "I can't lose you too, darlin." I asked, "Don't you wanna know where I was?" "We don't care since you're home now." After supper, I had to go to sleep. Before I left the room I heard Maw and Paw say, "We love you." That next mornin at break of day, I was out workin Pete's 10 acres.

4   We was going fast. The next thing I knew there was the Law behind us with flashing red and blue lights. The soldier stopped on the side of the road and said, "Be good. I was speeding." I never said nothin the whole time the soldier was talkin to the Law. Then the man asked me how I knew the soldier and I said, "I didn't." For some reason the Law said he had to give me a ride home. When we got there, he explained my story. Maw and Paw was real happy I was home. Pete wrote us a letter that said he was fine about a month later. We never heard from him again.

5   Then we was gone again. I looked over at the soldier next to me driving the car and wondered when Pete would get his soldier clothes. I could still feel where Pete kissed me. What got holt a him? Now we was back in the bus deepo and I was back in the middle of that mixup in Memphis. The soldier bought my ticket and asked again if I wanted a sandwich. "No sir. I jest got ta git home like Pete told me." Back on the bus again, I seen houses and houses. Will ever see Pete again?"

TWO SOLDIERS:
THE AUTHOR'S RESOLUTION

1. Then we was gone again. 2. And now I could see Memphis good, bright in the sunshine, while we was swinging around it. 3. And the first thing I knowed, we was back on the same highway the bus run on this morning—the patches of stores and them big gins and sawmills, and Memphis running on for miles, it seemed like to me, before it begun to give out. 4. Then we was running again between the fields and woods, running fast now, and except for that soldier, it was ike I hadn't never been to Memphis a-tall. 5. We was going fast now. 6. At this rate, before I knowed it we would be home again, and I thought about me riding up to Frenchman's Bend in this big car with a soldier running it, and all of a sudden I begun to cry. 7. I never knowed I was fixing to, and I couldn't stop it. 8. I set there by that soldier, crying. 9. We was going fast.

THE JILTING OF GRANNY WEATHERALL
LESSON PLAN 17

Film: "The Jilting of Granny Weatherall," The American Short Story Collection. Starring Geraldine Fitzgerald; 60 minutes. (AW Peller & Associates, 116 Washington Ave., PO Box 106, Hawthorne, NJ 07507-0106; www.awpeller.com)

Lesson 1: Reading and discussion of Porter's Granny Weatherall. (Plot-check quiz and discussion of a basic question).

Lesson 2: Make notations while viewing the film version of the story. Follow Film Guidelines (handout).

Lesson 3: Discussion of major film differences.

1. Focus: *Journal writing:* Have you ever seen a movie that inspired you to read the book upon which it was based? Have you ever been disappointed with a movie based on a book that you had already read?

2. Objective: To participate in a comparison-contrast discussion of the film version of the story and to write a follow-up comparison-contrast essay.

3. Purpose: To understand that film directors are presenting us with *their* interpretation of a written text.

4. Input: Plot-check quiz on the short story followed by discussion of a basic question of interpretation.

5. Modeling: Model some examples on overhead of writing differences between film and the original story (handout)

6. Checking for understanding: Review guidelines for making notations (handout).

7. Guided practice: Revise on overhead students' sentences on differences between film and text.

8. Closure: Comparison-contrast follow-up essay and/or movie review of the VHR.

Reading: Porter, Katherine Anne. "The Jilting of Granny Weatherall," in *Literature: An Introduction to Fiction, Poetry, and Drama.* X. J. Kennedy, Ed. 6th edition. New York, Harper Collins College Publishers, 1995, pp. 71–77.

THE JILTING OF GRANNY WEATHERALL:
REVISION EXERCISE

Directions: Write 10 complete sentences about differences or similarities between the movie and the original story. Use active voice. Avoid wordiness; be concise. Vary the sentence openings and mention both the movie and the short story in each sentence. (See p. 136.)

1. The movie starts with a flashback of George but the story starts with the doctor checking on Granny.

2. Granny was very active in the movie, when in the short story she just laid in bed.

3. In the movie, Granny is clearly in charge. The short story has her as being more passive.

4. Granny is up doing something although in the book she's in bed and can't move.

5. Galton was an added character.

6. The movie finally goes with the story about halfway through.

7. The story takes place in only one day, the movie in two.

8. Granny liked Hapsy the best because she had blonde hair.

9. Cornelia and Granny get in fights.

10. The beginning is different than in the movie.

11. In the story, she is more sickly, in the movie she can move around a lot.

12. While baking a cake Granny hears George whistling.

THE JILTING OF GRANNY WEATHERALL: SOME KEY MOVIE DIFFERENCES

1. During the entire short story, Granny is bedridden; in contrast, the movie covers the entire last day of her life.

2. In contrast to the short story, the movie has two additional characters—Jimmy, and Mr. Galton.

3. Unlike the short story, Granny tells Cornelia in the movie that God is as fickle as any human being and that work is the only certain thing that one can rely on.

4. The story begins with Doctor Harry's visit to Granny's bedside while the movie begins with a flashback to George.

5. Granny and Mr. Galton discuss death in the movie but not in the short story.

6. There are several direct confrontations between Cornelia and Granny in the movie; however, in the original story Granny keeps private her irritation with Cornelia's solicitations.

7. God takes the blame for Hapsy's premature death, according to the movie; in the short story, Granny's relationship with God is almost perfunctory.

8. Granny indirectly tells Cornelia about her first love, George, in the movie; in the short story she is careful to keep this part of her past life private.

9. "On Top of Old Smokey" provides background music in the movie unlike the short story.

10. The movie gives the impression that Granny is subconsciously reliving her wedding day when George jilted her; in contrast, in the short story all her memories of George are flashbacks.

11. The movie like the short story concludes with Granny blowing out the candle.

12. Granny directly confronts George in the movie but not in the short story.

13. The movie emphasizes Granny's control and willfulness more than does the short story.

14. Just as in the short story, in the movie Granny never did get over being jilted on her wedding day by George.

THE JILTING OF GRANNY WEATHERALL: COMPARISON/CONTRAST ESSAY—THINK SHEET

Purpose: To explain the significance of at least three important similarities or differences between the story and the film version.

Theses (choose one):

- ♦ Anyone who has read Porter's story will be disappointed with the film version.

- ♦ Anyone who has read Porter's story will be delighted with the film version.

- ♦ The film version of Porter's is so close to the plot and theme of the original that Porter herself could have directed its production.

Note: you must state *and* explain the significance of at least three important and specific differences *or* similarities between the movie and the short story. Attach your list of 10 similarities and/or differences to your final copy along with your first copy.

OF MICE AND MEN
LESSON PLAN 18

Lesson 1:   Reading and discussion of a basic question of *Of Mice and Men*. Plot-check quiz and discussion of a basic question.

Lesson 2:   Make notations while viewing the film version of the story. Follow Film Guidelines.

Lesson 3:   Discussion of a basic question of interpretation on the American dream.

1.	Focus:	Trivia quiz on the American dream.
2.	Objective:	To participate in a comparison-contrast discussion of three film clips of the story and to write a follow-up comparison-contrast essay.
3.	Purpose:	To realize that a film version of a story is the interpretation of the director with which the author may or may agree.
4.	Input:	Film versions of the novel: (1931) Burgess Meredith as George and Lon Chaney as Lennie (1985) Robert Blake as George and Randy Quaid as Lennie. (1992) Gary Sinise as George and John Malkovich as Lennie.
5.	Modeling:	*After viewing the film:* Model some examples on an overhead of how to write a few differences between the film and the story.
6.	Checking for understanding:	Review guidelines for writing differences between the film and the original story.
7.	Guided practice:	After viewing the film: Discussion of the significance of major differences between the three film clips and the story followed by discussion of a basic question: "According to Steinbeck, is the American dream an illusion or a realistic goal?"
8.	Closure:	Comparison-contrast follow-up essay and/or a movie review of the film (see Lesson 15 for guidelines).

Reading: Steinbeck, John (1972). *Of Mice and Men.* New York, Bantam Pathfinder.

OF MICE AND MEN:
LESSON 1—PLOT QUIZ
Chapters 1 and 2

Directions: These answers may be used once, more than once, or not at all since some are false and not all answers have been included. Write your answers on a separate sheet.

John Steinbeck	George Milton	Lennie Small
Carlson	Candy	Curley
Curley's wife	The boss	Slim
Crooks	He was caught stealing rabbits.	

"I don' like this place....This ain't no good place. I wanna get outa here."

He wanted to touch a girls dress and to pet it like a mouse.

To own a little farm, raise rabbits, and live "off the fatta the lan'."

If I was a relative of yours, I'd shoot myself."

"When are we gonna get there?"

To begin a new life in California.   To go to Alaska for gold.

He (1) was not "real bright"—in fact, he was retarded. He was a very large man who had the mind of a child and loved to pet soft, furry, things.

He (2) was a farmhand who had assumed the responsibility of taking care of another, unrelated, farmhand who kept getting into trouble.

He (3) was an old, crippled farmhand who had an old, lame sheepdog for a pet.

He (4) was a small, cocky, arrogant man who was a bully and former boxer.

He (5) was a tall, sympathetic farm hand who befriended George and Lennie. His word was law.

He (6) was "a pretty nice fella" who thought that George would probably steal Lennie's pay because he would not allow Lennie to speak for himself.

He (7) reprimanded this person (8) for staring at this person (9) who he also described as "jail bait," a "rat trap," and a "tart."

After the provocative appearance of this person (10), Lennie told George (11).

This (12) was the dream or plan of (13) and (14).

He (15) got into trouble in northern California (Weed) because he had (16).

He (17) was a powerful, big-stomached man who hated dogs.

He (18) was the stable buck who had been kicked by a horse. He read a lot.

He (19) repeatedly reminded him (20) that if he ever got into trouble, he was to hide in (21).

He (22) told him (23), "I got you to look after me, and you got me to look after you."

He (24) told George, "Ain't many guys travel around together. . . I don't know why."

George emphatically told Lennie to stay away from (25) and (26) because they could get them fired.

He (27) thought that he would probably have to "tangle" with him (28) sooner or later because (29).

Bonus point (30).

OF MICE AND MEN:
CHAPTERS 1 AND 2 PLOT QUIZ—ANSWER KEY

1.   Lennie

2.   George

3.   Candy

4.   Curley

5.   Slim

6.   The boss

7.   George

8.   Lennie

9.   Curley's wife

10.   Curley's wife

11.   "This ain't no good place."

12.   To own a little farm

13.   George

14.   Lennie

15.   Lennie

16.   tried to touch a girl's dress

117.   Carlson

8.   Crooks

19.   George

20.   Lennie

21.   the bush by the river.

22.   Lennie

23.   George

24.   Slim

25.   Curley

26.   Curley's wife

27.   George

28.   Curley

29–30.   George protected Lennie. Curley was a bully who hated "big guys."

SCORE: $30 \times 2 = 60$

Of Mice and Men:
Plot Quiz—Chapters 3 and 4

Directions: These answers may be used once, more than once, or not at all since some are false and not all answers have been included. Write your answers on a separate sheet.

John Steinbeck	George Milton	Lennie Small	Carlson
Candy	Curley	Curley's wife	The boss
Slim	Crooks	Whit	Clara
Andy Cushman	Heaven	Money in the bank	Friends

He (1) shot Candy's old, lame dog.

His (2) opinions were law because he was the (3).

He (4) had saved $350.00 that he wanted to use to buy into George and Lennie's dream.

He (5) was a young farm hand who wanted to know if his friend, Bill Tenner, has seen his letter to the editor in a pulp magazine.

This person (6) told this person (7), "I think you got your han' caught in a machine. If you don't tell nobody what happened, we ain't going to.

But you jus' tell an' try to get this guy (8) canned and we'll tell ever'body, an' then will you get the laugh."

He (9) wanted to cook and do odd jobs on George and Lennie's farm without pay. He first told his wish to (10) when they were alone in the bunkhouse.

During the same conversation, he (11) told (12) that "A guy needs somebody to be near him...A guy goes nuts if he ain't got nobody. Don't make no difference who the guy is, long's he's with you...I tell ya a guy gets too lonely an' he gets sick."

Curley's wife did believe that Curley's hand had been crushed in a machine because she saw it happen. (13) True or false. If false, explain.

This person (14) referred to this person (15) a "machine."

His (16) eyes were described as being "God-like."

He (17) got into a fight with this person (18) because he thought he was being laughed at by him.

This person (19) told this person (20), "I could get you strung up on a tree so easy it ain't even funny."

He (21) compared owning your own land to (22).

According to him (23), "Nobody gets to heaven, and nobody gets no land. It's just in their head."

He (24) became angry and upset when he found out that he (25) had told some of the other men about their dream.

OF MICE AND MEN:
CHAPTERS 3 AND 4 PLOT QUIZ—ANSWER KEY

1. Carlson

2. Slim

3. Foreman

4. Candy

5. Whit

6. Slim

7. Curley

8. Lennie

9. Crooks

10. Lennie

11. Crooks

12. Lennie

14. Curley's wife

15. Lennie

16. Slim

17. Lennie

18. Curley

19. Curley's wife

20. Crooks

21. Crooks

22. Heaven

23. Crooks

24. George

25. Lennie

13. False because he noticed marks on Lennie's face and called him a "machine."

SCORE: $25 \times 2 = 50$

OF MICE AND MEN:
PLOT QUIZ—CHAPTERS 5 AND 6

Directions: These answers may be used once, more than once, or not at all since some are false and not all answers have been included. Write your answers on a separate sheet.

John Steinbeck	George Milton	Lennie Small
Carlson	Candy	Curley
Curley's wife	The boss	Slim
Crooks	Aunt Clara	He killed a puppy.
He had stolen rabbits	Their dream farm	A giant rabbit
Bush by the river	Not fit to tend rabbits	Leave him
He would never own his own farm.		

He (1) worried that he (2) wouldn't let him tend the rabbits because (3).

He (4) was the first to discover the corpse of Curley's wife.

He (5) wanted to let Lennie escape after killing Curley's wife but he (6) wanted to have Lennie lynched. In fact, he wanted to shoot him himself.

After the death of Curley's wife, Cancy's greatest fear was (7).

Before George found Lennie in (8), Lennie imagined that he heard the voices of (9) and (10).

By having Lennie hear voices at this point in the story, Steinbeck is implying that Lennie did have a (11).

After the death of Curley's wife, Lennie heard someone (12) speaking to him: "I tol' you an' tol' you. I tol' you, 'Min' George because he's such a nice fella an' good to you.' But you don't take no care. You do bad things."

Another voice (13) told Lennie that he was (14) and that he (15) "was gonna beat hell outa" him and then that he was going to (16).

The men in the bunk house thought that he (17) had taken Carlson's Luger but he (18) had really taken it.

George allowed the farmhands believe that he (19) had taken Carlson's Luger because George needed time to (20).

When Curley discovered that George had killed Lennie, he was very angry because he had wanted to do it himself. (21) True or false. If false, explain.

When George finally found Lennie, he immediately "gave him hell" for "doing a bad thing." (22) True or false. If false, explain.

Lennie never did realize that George was going to kill him. (23) True or false. If false, explain.

Just before George killed Lennie, he talked about (24).

He (25) wanted him (26) to know that he had never been really angry with him for anything that he had done in the past.

He (27) alone assured George that he had done the right thing to kill Lennie.

The story concludes with this farmhand (28) asking another (29), "Now what the hell ya suppose is eatin' them two guys?"

George was arrested by the sheriff for the murder of Lennie. (30) True or false. If false, explain.

OF MICE AND MEN:
CHAPTERS 5 AND 6 PLOT QUIZ—ANSWER KEY

1. Lennie

2. George

3. He killed a puppy.

4. Candy

5. Candy

6. Curley

7. the loss of their farm

8. the bushes by the river

9. Aunt Clara

10. a giant rabbit

11. conscience or a sense of right and wrong.

12. Aunt Clara

13. a giant rabbit

14. not fit to tend rabbits

15. George

16. leave him

17. Lennie

18. George

19. Lennie

20. plan what to do about Lennie.

21. False. Curley was in awe that Lennie was dead already.

22. False. George knew it was too late to berate Lennie about anything. He felt only pity.

23. True

24. their dream of the farm

25. George

26. Lennie

27. Slim

28. Carlson

29. Curley

30. False. The story ends with Slim trying to console George.

SCORE: 30 × 2 = 60 possible points

OF MICE AND MEN:
THE AMERICAN DREAM TRIVIA QUIZ

1. According to this company, we can eat the American Dream!

2. What company claims that it has been "protecting" the American dream for over 50 years"?

3. What is the "American dream car"?

4. What newspaper says that it is "the daily diary of the American dream"?

5. Which NFL team as made a video entitled, "Living the American dream"?

6. Which Chicago newspaper claims that it is "the official sponsor of American dreams"?

7. According to this group of people, "where does the American dream begin"?

8. According to Lionel Trilling, what is "the only nation in the world that prides itself upon a dream and gives its name to one"?

9. What former coach of the Chicago Bears claims that he IS the American dream?

10. Which state license plate proclaims that it is "the land of opportunity"?

Answer Key

1. Edy's "American Dream" ice cream (vanilla)

2. Olympia Paints

3. Cadillac

4. The Wall Street Journal

5. The Dallas Cowboys

6. The Chicago Sun-Times

7. The National Education Association (NEA)

8. America (of course!)

9. Mike "Da Bears" Ditka

10. Arkansas

WHAT IS THE AMERICAN DREAM?

The American dream is:

◆ a BELIEF in the

◆ unlimited PROGRESS of all our citizens (who have been created equal, endowed by their Creator with the rights to life, liberty, and the pursuit of happiness)

♦ toward a goal of complete HAPPINESS (independence, individuality, wealth, success, power, fame, freedom, etc.)

♦ which was once attained in the PAST

♦ and which is attainable again in the FUTURE

♦ (if we make the effort),

♦ here on the Earth,

♦ in this Land, AMERICA!

THE AMERICAN DREAM

♦ "We hold these truths to be self-evident, that all men are created equal, that they are endowed by their Creator with certain unalienable rights, that among these are life, liberty, and *the pursuit of happiness*. That to secure these rights governments are instituted among men...that whenever any form of government becomes destructive of these ends, it is the right of the people to alter or to abolish it." — Thomas Jefferson, Declaration of Independence

♦ The phrase was first coined by James Truslow Adams in his *Epic of America* (1931): The American dream is "that dream of a better, richer, and happier life for all our citizens of every rank which is *the greatest contribution we have as yet made to the thought and welfare of the world*" (Preface, viii).

♦ The American dream "was *rebirth*, the eternal, haunting craving of men to be born again, the yearning for the second chance. The New World was that chance...its coat of arms bore and bears only one word—*Freedom*...the condition in which a man feels like a human being, like himself. It is the purpose, the definition, and consequence of rebirth. It is the Dream." — Eric Sevareid, "The American Dream"

♦ Essentially the American dream is as old as the mind of Man; we find it always in some country of the Western World. The Garden of Eden, Atlantis, Utopia, Brook Farm, etc.

♦ The discovery of the New World, the New Canaan (to the Puritans and Pilgrims), gave reality to the old myth and suggested the possible realization of it on earth, this is, in this New Land, America.

♦ "Ours is the only nation that prides itself upon a dream and gives its name to one—the American dream." — Lionel Trilling

♦ Each generation and nearly every author of American literature accepts the challenge to answer the basic question posed by the dream: "Is the American dream only a dream or is it a goal worth pursuing?"

OF MICE AND MEN:
BASIC QUESTIONS

BASIC QUESTION OF INTERPRETATION 1

According to Steinbeck, is the American dream an illusion that people foolishly pursue?

If *yes*, then:

1. Why does Steinbeck have George describe his and Lennie's dream in realistic, attainable terms? (pp. 16, 6)

2. Why does Steinbeck have Candy's money make George and Lennie's dream a real possibility? (pp. 65, 84)

3. Why does Steinbeck have the skeptic Crooks momentarily want to become part of George and Lennie's dream? (p. 84)

4. Why isn't George angry when he discovers that Lennie's accidental killing of Curley's wife means that they will never realize their dream? (pp. 104, 116–117)

5. Why does Steinbeck have owning their own farm mean independence for George and Candy? (pp. 63, 66)

If *no*, then:

6. Does Steinbeck have George and Lennie fail to achieve their dream because George never really believes in it? (p. 116)

7. Why does Steinbeck have Curley's wife fail to get to Hollywood? (p. 96)

8. Are we to conclude that George and Lennie's failure to reach their dream was merely "something that happened"? (original title of the novel)

9. Why DO the "best made plans of mind and men (sometimes) go astray? (actual title of the novel and allusion to Robert Burn's poem)

10. Does Steinbeck want us to believe that George relies too much on Lennie remembering what to do? (pp. 4, 17, 32, 60, 79, 81)

BASIC QUESTION INTERPRETATION 2

Why does Steinbeck have George and Lennie fail to achieve their idea of the American dream? *Restated:* According to the story, why do the best made plans of mice and men (title) sometimes go wrong?

1. Does Steinbeck want us to think that George depends too much on Lennie to do what he tells him to do? (pp. 32, 33, 60, 91)

2. Early in the story, why does George ignore Lennie's plea to "get outta here" because it was a "mean" place? (p. 36)

3. Why does Steinbeck emphasize that Lennie has trouble remembering things? (pp. 4, 17, 79)

4. Why does George go into town knowing that Lennie could get into trouble so easily when he was away? (p. 78)

5. Why doesn't George seem to realize that Lennie doesn't know the extent of his enormous strength?

6. Why does Steinbeck have the need for companionship lead to the destruction of Curley's wife and, as a result, to the destruction of Lennie? (p. 99)

7. Why is George so angry when he finds out that Lennie had told Candy and Crooks about their dream? (p. 91)

8. Why does Steinbeck have Crooks momentarily believe in George and Lennie's dream but then have him bitterly denounce it? (p. 84)

9. Why does Steinbeck have Candy want to buy into George and Lennie's dream? (pp. 65, 84)

10. After Curley's wife is dead, why does George think he has to kill Lennie? (p. 104)

11. Why does George finally admit that he knew "from the first" that he and Lennie would never achieve their dream? (p. 103)

12. Why isn't George angry when he discovers that Lennie's killing of Candy's wife means the end of their dream? (pp. 104, 116–117)

HAMLET
LESSON PLAN 19

FILM CRITICISM: "TO BE" SOLILOQUY [1.3.55–90]

1. Focus: *Journal writing:* Have you ever seen a movie that inspired you to read the book upon which it was based? Have you ever been disappointed with a movie based on a book that you had already read?

2. Objective: To participate in a comparison-contrast discussion of four film clips of the soliloquy and to write a follow-up comparison-contrast-persuasive essay to determine which actor gave the most understandable and convincing interpretation of the monologue.

3. Purpose: To understand that film directors are presenting us with their interpretation of a written text.

4. Input: View film clips of the four actors twice. Follow exactly guidelines for making notations.

5. Check for understanding: Review directions on film clip notation sheets.

6. Guided practice: Review and discuss notations after viewing film to develop ideas for follow-up essay.

7. Closure: Write a follow-up comparison-contrast-persuasive essay to determine which actor gave the most understandable and convincing interpretation of the soliloquy. Follow essay guidelines (handout) exactly.

Note: Two useful textbooks for writing about and discussing films based on novels, plays, or short stories are: (1) Costanzo, William. *Reading the Movies: Twelve Great Films on Video and How to Teach Them* (1992) and (2) Jan Bone and Ron Johnson, *Understanding the Film: An Introduction to Film Appreciation*, 5th edition (1997).

HAMLET:
FOUR ACTORS INTERPRET
"TO BE" SOLILOQUY [3.1.55–90]

Directions: As you view the film clip the first time, make notes on the setting and tone of each rendition. On the second viewing, make notes on key lines and gestures of each actor.

	Setting	Tone	Key Lines	Gestures
Lawrence Olivier (1948)				
Derek Jacobi (1985)				
Mel Gibson (1993)				
Kenneth Branagh (1996)				

HAMLET:
ESSAY GUIDELINES

Write a comparison-contrast essay to convince your reader that one of the four actors' interpretation of Hamlet's final soliloquy is better than the other two because it is more convincing and understandable.

1. Begin by making notations on the setting, tone, key lines, and gestures of each actor's presentation. See handout.

2. Rank the three interpretations in order of importance from most to least.

FIRST PARAGRAPH

3. Begin with your thesis (no introduction).

4. Explain why your top choice is best—your reasons along with specific supporting evidence.

SECOND PARAGRAPH

5. Counter argument (objection): why or how could someone else argue that your second choice should be first? Explain with reasons and supporting evidence.

6. Rebuttal

THIRD PARAGRAPH

7. Counter argument (objection): why could someone else argue that your third choice should be second? Explain with reasons and supporting evidence.

8. Rebuttal

9. Conclusion: restatement of your thesis.

MACBETH
LESSON PLAN 20

FILM CRITICISM: TOMORROW SOLILOQUY: 5.5.19–28

1. Focus:

Journal writing: Have you ever seen a movie that inspired you to read the book upon which it was based? Have you ever been disappointed with a movie based on a book that you had already read?

2. Objective:

To participate in a comparison-contrast discussion of four film clips of the soliloquy and to write a follow-up comparison-contrast-persuasive essay to determine which actor gave the most understandable and convincing interpretation of the monologue.

3. Purpose:

To understand that film directors are presenting us with their interpretation of a written text.

4. Input:

View film clips of the four actors twice. Follow exactly guidelines for making notations (handout).

5. Checking for understanding:

Review directions on film notation sheets.

6. Guided practice:

Review and discuss notations after viewing film to develop ideas for follow-up essay.

7. Closure:

Write a follow-up comparison-contrast-persuasive essay to determine which actor gave the most understandable and convincing interpretation of the soliloquy. Follow essay guidelines (handout) exactly.

Note: Two useful textbooks for writing about and discussing films based on novels, plays, or short stories are: (1) Costanzo, William. *Reading the Movies: Twelve Great Films on Video and How to Teach Them* (1992) and (2) Jan Bone and Ron Johnson, *Understanding the Film: An Introduction to Film Appreciation*, 5th edition (1997)

MACBETH:
FOUR ACTORS INTERPRET
"TOMORROW" SOLILOQUY [5.5.19–28]

Directions: As you view the film clip the first time, make notes on the setting and tone of each rendition. On the second viewing, make notes on key lines and gestures of each actor.

	Setting	Tone	Key Lines	Gestures
Jon Finch **(1985)**				
Orson Wells **(1948)**				
Michael Jayton **(1989)**				
Ian McKellen **(1976)**				

MACBETH:
ESSAY GUIDELINES

Write a comparison-contrast essay to convince your reader that one of the four actors' interpretation of Macbeth's final soliloquy is better than the other two because it is more convincing and understandable.

1. Begin by making notations on the setting, tone, key lines, and gestures of each actor's presentation. See handout.

2. Rank the three interpretations in order of importance from most to least.

FIRST PARAGRAPH

3. Begin with your thesis (no introduction).

4. Explain why your top choice is best—your reasons along with specific scenes.

SECOND PARAGRAPH

5. Counter argument (objection): why or how could someone else argue that your second choice should be first? Explain with reasons and supporting evidence.

6. Rebuttal

THIRD PARAGRAPH

7. Counter argument (objection): why could someone else argue that your third choice should be second? Explain with reasons and supporting evidence.

8. Rebuttal

9. Conclusion: restatement of your thesis.

FINDING FORRESTER
LESSON PLAN 21

Lesson 1:   View "Finding Forrester" part one (90 minutes).

Lesson 2:   "Finding Forrester" concluded (55 minutes) and prediscussion exercise on related follow-up questions (35 minutes).

Lesson 3:   Discussion of the basic question (45 minutes) and writing of a follow-up essay of resolution (45 minutes).

1. Focus:	*Journal writing:* commentary.In his book *On Writing*, Stephen King makes this astounding claim: "If I had not been able to make a career of writing, I am certain that alcohol and drugs would have been my end or I would have done some other vile thing like commit suicide."
2. Objective:	To view and participate in a discussion of "Finding Forrester" and to write a follow-up essay that is a comprehensive answer to a basic question of interpretation.
3. Purpose:	To increase our understanding, and, as a result our enjoyment of "Finding Forrester"—the story of how writing saved the lives of a 16-year-old teenager, Jamal Wallace, (Rob Brown) and a 70-year-old recluse, William Forrester (Sean Connery). MGM, 2001.
4. Input:	While viewing "Finding Forrester" (146 minutes) make notes on ten specific ways that Forrester helps Jamal to become a better writer.
5. Modeling:	At key moments, stop the film to ask students for specific examples of how Forrester is teaching Jamal to become a better writer.
6. Checking for understanding and guided practice:	Conduct a Socratic discussion of the film by asking follow- up questions of clarification, substantiation, consistency, and more opinion to resolve this basic question: *Does the title refer more to Forrester's helping Jamal to become a better writer or to Jamal's helping Forrester find himself?*
7. Closure:	Write a follow-up essay based on the class discussion that is each the student's individual and comprehensive answer to the basic question.

Note: In a block schedule of 90-minute periods, this lesson plan would have to be divided into a 3-day unit to view the film (146 minutes), to do the prediscussion exercise on related follow-up questions (20 minutes), to participate in discussion (55 minutes), and to write a follow-up essay of 1000 words (40 minutes). In a schedule of 55-minute periods, the lesson plan would take 5 days (275 minutes).

FINDING FORRESTER

Film: 146 minutes; Sean Connery as William Forrester and Rob Brown as Jamal Wallace

A Basic Question of Interpretation

Does the title, "Finding Foorester," refer more to Forrester's helping Jamal become a better writer or Jamal's helping Forrester find himself?

Prediscussion Exercise

Directions: At the left of each question, mark *FO* if the question is directly related Forrester helping Jamal, *JA* if the question is related to Jamal helping Forrester, and *NR* if the question is related to neither side of the issue.

_____ 1. During an English class on Poe's "The Raven," why does Jamal refuse to recite by saying that he had not read the poem?

_____ 2. Why is Mrs. Wallace told by Jamal's English teacher that her son is a C student with an A on the state assessment test?

_____ 3. Why did Jamal turn to reading and writing after his father abandoned his family?

_____ 4. Does Jamal's peer acceptance depend entirely on basketball?

_____ 5. Why does the film contrast the accomplishments of Jamal's gregarious brother, Terral, with Jamal's aspirations?

_____ 6. When Jamal finds his backpack in the street, why does he discover comments in red ink in his journals?

_____ 7. In one of his red-ink comments, why does Forrester ask Jamal, "Where are you taking me"?

_____ 8. By "constipated thinking," does Forrester mean that Jamal's writing is not clear?

_____ 9. When Jamal first knocks on Forrester's door, why does he take up the challenge to write 5000 words on why he should stay away?

_____ 10. After professor Crawford tells his students that William Forrester wrote a masterpiece at 23, why is his first assignment to find out why Forrester wrote only one book rather than questions about the book itself?

_____ 11. When Jamal asks Forrester why he is a legend at school, why does Forrester shout at him, "The purpose of a question is to obtain information *that matters to you*"?

_____ 12. Why does Forrester tell Jamal he will go to Maylor because he wants to answer the question about what he will do with the rest of his life?

_____ 13. When Forrester asks Jamal if he had read his only book, *Avalon Landing*, why does Jamal say he couldn't get past the first ten pages?

_____ 14. Why does Forrester not want anyone to know about Jamal's visits to his apartment?

_____ 15. When Jamal asks if Forrester will keep helping him with his writing, why does Forrester agree only if Jamal asks no questions about him, his family, or why he wrote only one book?

_____ 16. What does Forrester mean when he tells Jamal, "People are always *talking* about my book but never *saying* anything about it"?

_____ 17. When Jamal tells Forrester that his book means that "Life never works out," why does Forrester reply that he didn't have to read a book to learn that?

_____ 18. What does Forrester mean when he says that "The first step to writing is writing—not thinking about what you are going to write"?

_____ 19. What does Forrester mean when he says to write the first draft with your heart but then to rewrite with your head"?

_____ 20. How does Forrester's having Jamal type out a copy of his "A Season of Faith's Perfection" help Jamal to "discover his own words"?

_____ 21. Why does Forrester insist that whatever he and Jamal write must stay in his apartment?

_____ 22. Why does Forrester warn Jamal that "Bitterly disappointed teachers [of writing like Robert Crawford] are either very good or very dangerous"?

_____ 23. When Jamal gives Clare the unexpected gift of a signed copy of Forrester's book, why does she ask if he had been trying to show her more than how to dribble a basketball?

_____ 24. Did Forrester write only one book mostly because he so profoundly resents critics who try to explain what he was "really" trying to say or because of his brother's untimely death?

_____ 25. Why does Jamal take Forrester to a stadium on his birthday?

_____ 26. After Forrester tells Jamal about his brother's drunk-driving death, why does Jamal quote Forrester's words, "The rest of those who have gone before us cannot study the unrest of those who follow"?

_____ 27. What has Jamel learned from Forrester and Forrester from Jamel?

_____ 28. When Jamal realizes that Forrester will not defend him publicly, is he serious giving up writing?

_____ 29. Why is Jamal presented with the choice of winning a championship to retain his scholarship?

____ 30. Why does Jamal ignore Forrester's question about the missed fowl shots?

____ 31. When Jamal goes to the writing contest awards, why does he tell Clare that Maylor will have to kick him out of school—that he will not just walk away?

____ 32. Why does Forrester come out of retirement to defend Jamal?

____ 33. How did Jamal's writing contest entry, "Loosing Family," make Forrester realize that "the one wish that [he] was granted so late in life was the gift of friendship"?

____ 34. Even after Forrester convincingly demonstrates that Jamal's "Losing Family" was his own work, why does Professor Crawford still want Jamal disqualified?

____ 35. Why is Professor Crawford over ruled and Forrester offered a teaching job?

____ 36. After his death from cancer, why does Forrester want Jamal to have his apartment?

____ 37. In his final letter to Jamal, what does Forrester mean when he says, "I never imagined that I would realize my own dream once again"?

____ 38. Why does Forrester credit Jamal's coming into his life for realizing his dream so late in life?

____ 39. Why does Forrester leave to Jamal the manuscript of *Sunset* with "the forward to be written by Jamal Wallace"?

____ 40. How does the story's resolution imply that Jamel will become one day a successful writer?

Answer Key

Questions directly related to Forrester (FO) helping Jamal become a better writer: 6–9, 11, 12, 14–22, 24, 32, 33, 36–40.

Questions directly related to Jamal (JA) helping Forrester find himself: 13, 24, 25, 26, 27, 28, 29, and 31.

Questions not related (NR) to either side of the issue: 1-5, 10, 23, 30, 34, and 35.

6

THE WHAT, WHY, AND HOW OF LITERATURE CIRCLES

TWELVE PRINCIPLES OF LITERATURE CIRCLES

Literature Circles are a natural follow-up to Socratic discussion because they also strive to develop independent and reflective thinking. The major difference between the Circles and discussion is that the leader's role in Literature Circles is divided into several distinct roles. On the other hand, in both activities the goal is the same—to increase understanding (comprehension), and as a result, enjoyment of the story so that kids learn how to get into books and become life-long readers.

The first time I saw Harvey Daniels speak was in a large conference room in Wheaton, Illinois. His discussion centered of the nature of reading and how it should develop a sense of the human condition. The teachers I remember most are those who had the ability and courage to tap into the things that really move us: love, relationships, fears, pain, hopes and dreams. Some teachers, perhaps subconsciously, seem to have been taught to restrict, ignore, or dismiss, the human element in their classrooms. I agree strongly with Daniels' position on the relationship between reading and the human spirit, "We've asked kids to bottle up their responses, and in doing so we have blocked the pathway that leads upward from responding to analyzing and evaluating" (*Literature Circles: Voice and Choice in the Student-Centered Classroom*, 9). With mock humor and irony, Daniels correctly pointed out that presently, "traditional school reading programs are virtually designed to ensure that kids never voluntarily pick up a book once they graduate."(Daniels, 11.)

Two key concepts associated with Literature Circles are independent reading and collaborative learning that were first developed by Becky Abraham Searle. Today, her idea, like Harvey Daniels', is being developed and adapted with great enthusiasm throughout the country. So what are the characteristics of an authentic Literature Circle? At some point in their development, these *twelve principles* will be implemented:

- *First*, students choose their own reading.

- *Second*, small temporary groups are formed based on book choice.

- *Third*, different groups read different books.

- *Fourth*, groups meet on a regular, predictable schedule for discussion.

- *Fifth*, kids use written notes to guide both their reading and discussion.

- *Sixth*, discussion topics come from the students, not the teacher.

- *Seventh*, group meetings strive to become open, *natural* conversations about books.

- *Eighth*, students take on a rotating tasks of distinct of roles.

- *Ninth*, the teacher serves as a facilitator and not as a group member or instructor.

- *Tenth*, evaluation is by teacher observation and student self-evaluation.

- *Eleventh*, a spirit of fun about reading pervades the room.

- *Twelfth*, when books are finished, readers share with their classmates and new groups form around new reading choices (Daniels, 18).

Several of these principles need elaboration. On the *first* principle of letting children choose their own reading, some veteran English teachers may gasp. However, I am not old enough to gasp but agree with Daniels' contention that "you absolutely can not fall in love with a book that someone stuffs down your throat" (19). In my classroom students are allowed to choose from the books that we have available or are easily obtainable and meet in groups of four or five with those who have chosen the same book.

Principle *two,* that groups form around book choice is also vital. I want to group kids the way they would naturally group themselves—out of a common interest. I also realize that I may start off the class with every student picking one book to read for themselves on their own with a regularly scheduled Friday for sustained silent reading, just to get them into the mode of reading for pleasure on their own. Later, I get kids into Literature Circles with a limited list of books from which they can choose and want to read in a group setting. While there is an initial challenge in letting kids choose their own books and groups, this difficulty can soon be overcome by trial-and-error and common sense.

The *third* principle of allowing kids to choose their books is important for two reasons: It gives them the opportunity to assign reading to themselves as adults do. By giving students the opportunity and practice of setting up their own readings they take ownership of reading. With practice and repetition it may continue even after they leave school. Second, choice is an integral part of literate behavior. Being forced to read too often results in not reading at all—even when one has the freedom to do so.

The *fourth* principle is to have discussions on a regular and predictable schedule. As Daniels states, "literature circles require a consistent down payment of time for training, but once they are installed in your portfolio of strategies, they pay big dividends in the reading program all year long" (21). At times, my students meet in Literature Circles weekly, biweekly, or monthly.

The *fifth* principle that kids use written notes to guide both their reading and discussion is essential for the success of the program. By using role sheets (explanation to follow), students have time to respond to the reading before discussion to be able to bring something specific to discussion. Instead of having students fill in correct phrases or answers in workbooks, Literature Circles allows students to reflect and write down their responses *before* discussion. In this way they become genuinely active readers. In addition to preparing students for discussion, notes gathered from these role-playing sheets also serve as a staging area of ideas in the book. These notes can be used by the group for a follow-up project that summarizes main ideas and themes in creative ways: book reviews, advertising posters, "missing chapters," or converting parts into readers' theater. As a result, students often interest other students in their book.

Principle *six*, that discussion topics come from the students themselves, is also crucial. Indeed, this may be the most important feature of all: "After all, if kids never practice digging the big ideas out of texts themselves and always have teachers doing it for them, how can they ever achieve literary and intellectual independence?" (23). This condition should not be confused with permissiveness or letting kids do whatever they want. When kids are given the opportunity *and* the challenge (thinking *is* difficult) to ask what is really bothering them, they begin to ask *real* questions—those that they have no answer to at all or those that evoke several answers but none entirely satisfy. Only real questions lead to an increase in understanding and comprehension.

Principle *eight*, that students play a rotating assortment of task roles provides the structure for students to be free to examine their responses. Since a goal of this kind of discussion is to develop individual responsibility, students must clearly understand the varied roles or tasks they will assume. These roles should be structured enough so the student is aware of what he or she is going to be doing but not so structured as to have a specific outcome in mind.

Open-endedness is crucial for lasting results. Daniels stresses that roles rotate so each student has an opportunity to approach the books from different angles. This gives them chances to internalize the various perspectives offered from each role. Incidentally, he also advises that once all the students virtually have all of the different roles mastered or memorized that they be phased out and led into using only their personal response logs (25).

Number *nine*, that the teacher serves as a "facilitator" sounds like a cliche but not for Daniels. In this setting the teacher's role is not to dispense correct answers but to organize, manage, and handle the logistics. This involves collecting sets of good books, helping groups form, visiting and observing meetings, conferring with kids or groups who struggle, orchestrating shared sessions, keeping records, making assessment notes, and collecting more books for them to read (26).

Principle *ten*, evaluation both by teacher observation and student self-evaluation, implies that covering material, teaching specific subskills, or being sure they get it (that is, the "correct" interpretation) are all beside the point. According to Daniels, "Literature circles necessitate high-order assessment of kids working at the whole thing, the complete, put-together outcome—which, in this case, is joining in a thoughtful small-group conversation about literature" (27). Here authentic assessment by the teacher is through postdiscussion critiques (when the teacher points out what was done well and why and what needs improvement and how to do it), kid watching, narrative observational logs, performance assessment, checklists, student conferences, group interviews, video/audio taping, and collecting materials produced in the end-of-the-book group project. Equally important, students are responsible for writing a personal assessment of their own role(s) in the group, record-keeping and written summaries and/or resolutions to the discussion questions.

Principle *eleven*, that a spirit of playfulness and fun pervade the room, may be a red flag to some principals and teachers, but not to me. I know the things I learned the most from were almost universally the most fun. In my seventh grade social studies class I was very much involved in the various projects and competitions that made learning fun. In these Literature Circles I want create a sense that what they are doing is enjoyable. The fun parts are there. They get to choose the books, thereby choosing the groups. They get to choose roles that are varied and temporary. They get to talk with their friends about what they are reading. They get to design their own "cool" end-of-the-book project that makes the book come alive for them. And then they get to change the book and start all over again.

The *twelfth* principle bears repeating. New groups form around new reading material. There is a constant mixing in the classroom as different combinations of children are thrown together with each new book choice. This, in effect, may break up groups that have become quite comfortable with each other but I think

it is in the best interest of the class to shuffle the groups for developing important social skills and ultimately building a real sense of community. In addition,
when kids choose their books, they are detracking themselves and the leveling
is self-chosen, temporary, and within a mixed class. In essence Literature Circles
help make ability grouping unnecessary (29). On the other hand, what can be
done when a student chooses a book that is too hard for his or her level? Daniels
has two suggestions: the teacher has a private reading conference with the student to select another book or to provide help (an aide, peer helper, or parent to
read parts aloud or even getting the book on tape if possible) necessary for the
student to achieve enough understanding to be able to function in his or her
group (183).

THE FUNCTION OF
ROLE SHEETS IN DISCUSSION

For many teachers who have implemented Literature Circles, four key roles
are *required* for success: Discussion Leader, Passage Master, Connector, and a
Wordsmith. Optional roles (for groups larger than four) are illustrator, summarizer, character captain, and the scene setter. To illustrate the importance and
function of the first four roles, I spend two days modeling each task on a selection (for example, Robert Frost's "The Road Not Taken") that the entire class has
read to make sure students understand what they will be asked to do in their
own groups (153–157).

The job of the *Discussion Leader* is to develop a list of questions that the group
might want to discuss about the section of the book that is to be read prior to
their meeting. It is vital that the teacher explain, illustrate, and test student understanding about the difference between the *three kinds of questions:* factual, interpretive, and evaluation. (See Lesson Plan 1, pp. 26–29. See also Lesson Plan 2
(pp. 32–35), on the qualities of good prepared questions, and Lesson Plan 3
(pp. 42–48), on spontaneous follow-up questions.)

Unless the Discussion Leader understands that he is being asked to write
and lead the discussion with *interpretive* questions, there can be *no increase* in
understanding of the book. Discussion dead-ends when factual questions are
raised since they have but one correct answer. Questions of evaluation, those
based on personal experience or values, are raised by the Connector, *not* the Discussion Leader.

The job of the *Passage Master* is to locate a few special passages of the text
that the person thinks the group would like to hear read aloud. The idea here is
to help people remember some interesting, powerful, funny, puzzling, or important section(s) of the text. This person's role also involves reading the passage aloud to the group, explaining why he or she picked it, and what he or she
plans to look for related to it as the reading progresses (78.)

Each group should also have a *Wordsmith* who selects in advance several especially important words that appeared in the reading. These words may be puzzling or unfamiliar, or familiar words that stand out because they are often repeated, used in an unusual way, or are key to the meaning of the text. For example, in Jack Schaefer's classic Western, *Shane*, the word *man* appears 122 times. In nearly every context, it means more than male.

Finally, the *Connector's* role is to find connections between the book the group is reading and the world outside. This means connecting the reading to their lives, to happenings at school or in the community, to similar events at other times and places, or to other people or problems that the Connector is reminded of (80).

For teachers who first introduce their students to Literature Circles, a common concern is logistical. For example, a local middle school teacher has written:

> If I do writers workshop four days a week and literary circles every Friday I'm concerned students may be too rushed, or there may be too much time in between group meetings. As a result, at the outset I will allow more time for training and practice until I'm certain they have the hang of it. Once the roles are familiar and established, I think I can turn them over to developing reading schedules that have them reading four days out of five and meeting with lots to talk about on that Friday regarding their books. My final logistical concern is the garnering of the books to be used for this project. I have a good number of books at my disposal however I am sure I do not have enough. I think possibly I can get parents to subsidize the cost of books if they could contribute a few dollars for them. Also the PTA is very active and generous in the school and perhaps they would be willing to contribute funds for book purchases. I will see how that all goes as the year progresses.

PREPARING STUDENTS TO PARTICIPATE IN LITERARY CIRCLES LESSON PLAN 22

ROLE SHEETS ON *BETHGELERT*

1. Focus:

    When was the last time you really discussed a book with a friend? What was the title? Why did you want to talk about that book?

2. Objective:

    To understand the nature and requirements of the four roles that participants share in small-group discussions.

3. Purpose:

    To prepare you for *four different role tasks* that you will be asked to perform at different times when you get together with your discussion groups.

4. Input & modeling:

    First reading (oral) of *Bethgelert;* second reading (silent): make notations on whatever is important, whatever you don't understand, whatever you like or dislike, agree or disagree with, or whatever is related—one part of the story to another.

5. Checking:

    Review the directions on each of the four handouts: Discussion Leader, Passage Master, Wordsmith, and Connector.

6. Guided practice:

    Divide class into groups of four assigning each group one of the four tasks.

7. Closure:

    Review each groups' findings for each of the four roles.

BETHGELERT
BY WILLIAM SPENCER, 1811

Prince Llewelyn had a favorite greyhound named Gellert that had been given to him by his father-in-law, King John. He was as gentle as a lamb at home, but a lion in the chase. One day, Llewelyn went to the chase and blew his horn in front of his castle. All his other dogs came to the call, but Gellert never answered it. So he blew a louder blast on his horn and called Gellert by name, but still the greyhound did not come. At last, Prince Llewelyn could wait no longer and went off to the hunt without Gellert. He had little sport that day because Gellert was not there, the swiftest and boldest of his hounds.

He turned back in a rage to his castle, and as he came to the gate, who should he see but Gellert come bounding out to meet him. But when the hound came near him, the Prince was startled to see that his lips and fangs were dripping with blood. Llewelyn started back and the greyhound crouched down at his feet as if surprised or afraid at the way his master greeted him.

Now Prince Llewelyn had a little son a year old with whom Gellert used to play, and a terrible thought crossed the Prince's mind that made him rush towards the child's nursery. And the nearer he came, the more blood and disorder he found about the room. He rushed into it and found the child's cradle overturned and daubed with blood.

Prince Llewelyn grew more and more terrified, and sought for his little son everywhere. He could find him nowhere but only signs of some terrible conflict in which much blood had been shed. At last he felt sure the dog had destroyed his child, and shouting to Gellert, "Monster, thou hast devoured my child," he drew out his sword and plunged it into the greyhound's side, who fell with a deep yelp and still gazing in his master's eyes.

As Gellert raised his dying cry, a little child's cry answered it from beneath the cradle, and there Llewelyn found his child unharmed and just awakened from sleep. But just beside him lay the body of a great gaunt wolf all torn to pieces and covered with blood. Too late, Llewelyn learned what had happened while he was away. Gellert had stayed behind to guard the child and had fought and slain the wolf that had tried to destroy Llewelyn's heir.

In vain was all Llewelyn's grief; he could not bring his faithful dog to life again. So he buried him outside the castle walls within sight of the great mountain of Snowdon, where every passer-by might see his grave, and raised over it a great cairn of stones. And to this day, the place is called, Beth Gellert, or the Grave of Gellert, and men say, *"I repent me as much as the man that slew his greyhound."*

Sources: Spencer, W. (1998). "Bethgelert," in *Celtic Fairy Tales*. Bristol, England: Paragon. Internet: http://www.pitt.edu/`dash/type0178a.html

HANDOUTS FOR LITERATURE CIRCLES

REQUIRED ROLE SHEETS

- *Discussion Leader:* prepares at least five interpretive questions before discussion and asks spontaneous follow-up questions during discussion. The leader also invites each member of the group to contribute what he or she has prepared (passages, vocabulary, and connections).

- *Passage Master:* selects and reads aloud at least three key passages from the assigned reading, explains why those passages were chosen and then raises questions about them.

- *Wordsmith:* selects at least five important or unusual vocabulary words and bring them up during discussion when related.

- *Connector:* prepares at least *four questions of evaluation*—two based on experience and two based on personal values.

Note: See Chapter 5 of *Literature Circles* for an explanation of sample role sheets.

DISCUSSION LEADER

Name _____   Date _____

Group _____   Class _____

Book _____   Author _____

Assignment: pp. _____ to _____

Discussion Leader: Your job *before* meeting with your group is to prepare a list of five good interpretive questions for discussion. (The best questions usually come from your thoughts, feelings, and concerns as you read the story. Whenever possible, add a page for the reference that made you think of each question.) Your task during discussion is to help your group reflect on, share, and develop its own responses to the reading. You do this during discussion by asking good spontaneous follow-up questions for clarification, substantiation, and for more opinion. During discussion you should also invite each member to contribute the part that he or she has prepared for discussion: important passages, vocabulary, and connections.

Five Prepared Interpretive Questions for Discussion

1. _____

2. _____

3. _____

4. _____

5. _____

After discussion, list below any questions left over that could be carried over to the next group meeting:

1. _____

2. _____

3. _____

PASSAGE MASTER

Name _____   Date _____

Group _____   Class _____

Book _____   Author _____

Assignment: pp. _____ to _____

Passage Master: Your job is to locate at least four special sections of the reading that you think your group ought to read aloud and focus its discussion on. Your job is to help your group focus on several interesting, powerful, funny, puzzling, or important passages of the story. You decide which passages or paragraphs are worth hearing and then make a note on how to share them. You can read passages aloud yourself or ask someone else to read them. After the oral reading, ask each member of the group a question about the passage.

Location   **Reason(s) for Choosing This Passage**

1. Page _____

Paragraph _____

2. Page _____

Paragraph _____

3. Page _____

Paragraph _____

4. Page _____

Paragraph _____

Possible Reasons for Picking a Passage to Share with Your Group

Important	Informative	Surprising	Controversial
Funny	Well written	Confusing	Memorable
Touching	It is so true	It is so false	Thought-provoking

CONNECTOR

Name _____   Date _____

Group _____   Class _____

Book _____   Author _____

Assignment: pp. _____ to _____

Connector: Your job is to find connections between the book your group is reading and the world outside. List below at least four questions of evaluation that connect the reading to your life, to happenings at school or in the community, to similar events at other times and places, to other people, or to problems that you are reminded of. You may also see connections between this book or to others on the same topic or by the same author. Whatever connections you make with the reading based on your own experience or values is what you ought to share with your group.

Questions of Evaluation Based on Personal Experience

1. _____

2. _____

Questions of Evaluation Based on Personal Values

3. _____

4. _____

List Below Any Questions of Evaluation Left Over after Discussion

5. _____

6. _____

WORDSMITH

Name _____   Date _____

Group _____   Class _____

Book _____   Author _____

Assignment: pp. _____ to _____

Vocabulary Enricher: Your job is to put your finger on at least five especially important words in today's reading. If you find words that are puzzling or unfamiliar, mark them while you are reading and then later jot down their definitions, either from a dictionary or some other source. You may also select familiar words that stand out somehow in the reading—words that are repeated often, used in an unusual way, or are key to the meaning of the story. Mark these special words and bring them up during your group discussion whenever they seem related.

Page and

	Paragraph	Word	Definition
1.	_____	_____	_____
2.	_____	_____	_____
3.	_____	_____	_____
4.	_____	_____	_____
5.	_____	_____	_____
6.	_____	_____	_____
7.	_____	_____	_____
8.	_____	_____	_____

OPTIONAL ROLE SHEETS

Optional role sheets encompass the roles of:

- ◆ Illustrator

- ◆ Summarizer

- ◆ Travel Tracer

- ◆ Researcher

Note: See Chapter 5 of *Literature Circles* for an explanation of sample role sheets.

ASSESSMENT OF LITERATURE CIRCLES

How does a teacher know if kids are learning in literature circles? How can these discussions be evaluated? According to Harvey Daniels (*Literature Circles*, 1994) we have to begin with these questions:

1. What are we assessing for?

2. When we observe, record, measure, or judge, what are we trying to accomplish?

3. What theories and principles guide our assessment efforts? (p. 159)

To answer these questions, three major guiding principles should be (1) To reinforce *learner-centered* teaching methods. (2) To make assessment *an integral part of instruction,* not some-thing separate from teaching or done only after teaching. (3) To use a *variety of assessment strategies* and not be limited by traditional norm-referenced, competitive measures that rank students one against another. In short, authentic assessment should be *formative* not merely a judgment call.

Given these Guidelines, *in what specific ways* can teachers assess students in literature circles? Several come to mind: student behaviors during discussion, checklists, interviews, conferences, worksheets, and follow-up writing assignments.

1. *Observation* of student behaviors during discussion. Keyed either to the role sheets for a given discussion or to names of students in the small groups, *checklists* are an important observational tool. Another tool is to develop a rubric of formal performance criteria and use a scaled score sheet to rate the entire group's performance. For a model, see the "Criteria for Critique of Discussion" employed in Socratic Seminars (Chapter 4, p. 55).

2. Individual *Reading Conferences* also enable a teacher to assess the value of literature circles. Here "Teachers can talk with the students about their own role in the group, the circle's problems and pleasures, and about the group's handling of specific books and ideas" (p. 163). An alternative is to conduct group conferences with each literature circle that enable teachers and students to reflect on what has or has not been accomplished.

3. *Portfolios* are also an important means of overall assessment because they include everything related to the reading and discussion of a book: daily role sheets, reading journals, and whatever extended, follow-up activity culminates the reading and discussions. For

some teachers the most important elements here is a formal essay on an assigned or student chosen topic.

4. The role sheets help set students' purposes for reading that guide the group meetings are *artifacts* teachers can collect to evaluate the level of individual effort and performance.

5. Some kind of *culminating project* is yet another way to synthesize what has been learned by individual students and to promote the book among other students in the class so that they may consider choosing the reading for one of their groups.

Finally, Harvey Daniels proposes the following evaluation form for literature circles:

Literature Circles Evaluation Form

%	Trait	Source of Data
40%	*Productivity*	
	Quantity of reading	Daily role sheets
	Preparation for discussion	Teacher observation
	Contributions to group	
40%	*Growth*	
	Variety of books, authors, genres	Daily role sheets
	Explanations and interpretations	Conferences
	Use of input from peers/teacher	Teacher observation
	Application of news skills and to next book	Artifacts
	Response expressed in projects	Projects
20%	*Quality of Reading*	
	Difficulty of texts read	Teacher observation
	Level of thinking shown	Conferences
	Leadership in group sessions	Artifacts
	Sophistication of projects	Portfolios

Note: In this scoring scale, the grade is derived from three ingredients: productivity, growth, and quality. The first two criteria, totaling 80 percent of the grade, are self-referenced measures—they compare the kid to self, not others. The other 20 percent—the "quality" assessment—*is* a norm-referenced measure, which basically says, "Compared to the rest of the kids; in this class, the level of this child's reading/thinking ability is so-and-so" (p. 167).

REFERENCES

Active Learning Practices for Schools. *The thinking classroom* http://learnweb.harvard.edu/alps/thinking/index.cfm

Adler, M. J. (1955). *A guide for leaders of great books discussion groups.* Chicago: Great Books Foundation.

Adler, M. J. (1991). *Introducing the Socratic seminar into the elementary school classroom.* Chicago: Chicago Public Schools.

Adler, M. J. (1982). *The Paideia proposal: An educational manifesto.* New York: Macmillan.

Adler, M. J. (1984) *The Paideia program.* New York: Macmillan.

Adler, M.J. (1977). *Reforming education: The opening of the American mind.* New York: Macmillan.

Adler, M.J. (1940). *How to mark a book.* The Saturday Review (July 6).

Adler, M.J. (1940). *How to read a book: The art of getting a liberal education.* New York: Simon & Schuster.

Barthes, R. (1983). Sontag, S. (Ed.). *A Barthes reader.* New York: Noonday Press.

Bloom, B. (Ed.). (1956) *Taxonomy of educational objectives.* New York: McKay.

Bone, Jan and Ron Johnson. (1997). *Understanding the film: An introduction to film appreciation*, 5th edition.

Brunner, J. (1960). *The process of education.* New York: Alfred A. Knopf, Inc.

Canady, R. & Rettig, M. (1999). *Teaching in the block: Strategies for engaging active learners.* Larchmont, NY: Eye on Education.

Christenbury, L. & Kelly, P. (1983). *Questioning: A path to critical thinking.* Urbana, IL: National Council of Teachers of English.

Costanzo, W. (1992). *Reading the movies: Twelve great films on video and how to teach them.* Urbana, IL: National Council of Teachers of English.

Daniels, H. (1994). *Literature circles: Voice and choice in the student-centered classroom.* York, ME: Stenhouse Publishers.

Frye, N. (1970). *The educated imagination.* Bloomington: Indiana University Press.

Golub, J. (Ed.). (1986) *Activities to promote critical thinking: Classroom practices in teaching English.* Urbana, IL: National Council of Teachers of English.

McMahan, Elizabeth, et. al. (1988*). The elements of writing about literature and film.* New York: Macmillan Publishers.

Mitchell, R. (1979). *Less words can say.* Boston: Little, Brown and Company.

Morris, E. (1998) *The book lover's guide to the Internet.* New York: Fawcett Columbine.

National Council for Excellence in Critical Thinking. "Why teach Socratically?" http://www.criticalthinking.org/ncect.ncik

Neilson, A. R. (1989). *Critical thinking and reading*. Urbana, IL: National Council of Teachers of English.

Provenzo, E. (1998). *The educator's brief guide to the World Wide Web*. Larchmont, NY: Eye on Education.

Romano, T. (1995). *Clearing the way: Working with teenage writers*. Dallas, TX: Heinemann.

Rouse, W. H., (Trans.). (1956) *The great dialogues of Plato*. New York: Mentor.

Reddick, R & King, B. (1996*) The online student: Making the grade on the Internet*. New York: Harcourt Brace.

Silberman, M. (1996) *Active learning: 101 strategies to teach any subject*. Boston: Allyn and Bacon.

Strong, W. (1994). *Sentence Combining: A Composing Book*. 3rd ed. New York: McGraw-Hill, Inc.

Strong, W. (1996). *Writers toolbox: A sentence combining workshop*. New York: McGraw-Hill, Inc.

Warren, R. & Wellek, W., (1956). *Theory of literature*. New York: Harcourt, Brace and Company.

Whitehead, A. N. (1929). *The aims of education*. New York: Macmillan Co.